Silva
UltraMind
SYSTEMS

ESP
FOR
BUSINESS
SUCCESS

Silva
UltraMind
SYSTEMS

ESP
FOR
BUSINESS
SUCCESS

JOSÉ SILVA JR.
KATHERINE SANDUSKY
ED BERND JR.

MEDIA

Published 2019 by Gildan Media LLC
aka G&D Media
www.GandDmedia.com

Front Cover design by David Rheinhardt of Pyrographx

Interior design by Meghan Day Healey of Story Horse, LLC.

Library of Congress Cataloging-in-Publication Data
is available upon request

ISBN: 978-1-7225-1006-0

10   9   8   7   6   5   4   3   2   1

Contents

Part Two
How to Use Your Mind to Increase Productivity

Foreword

by Chris Downes

Statistically I had no hope of achieving anything. Yet I have had a very successful life. I had a very successful 30-year career in the British police service. I've had a long and loving marriage and family life too.

How did that happen to a person who was born into a poor community in the north of England 69 years ago, whose father died when he was three, and who left school at age 15 with no qualifications?

How did I become a senior officer in the British police service? How did I achieve a master's degree in education? How did I become an accredited training evaluator in the government department responsible for policing in Great Britain?

You are holding the answer to these and many other questions in your hands. I was one of the "naturals," one of the 10 percent of humanity who somehow grow up retaining the ability to use effective sensory projection (ESP) naturally.

This is not just another book to read. I consider this the most advanced training program for anyone who wants to be the best in their chosen field. It will show you exactly how to develop the ability that only one person in 10 develops naturally: the ability to detect information with your mind, to make better decisions, and to attract good luck and beneficial coincidences.

My life has been full of what I thought were coincidences.

I had a wonderful 30 years in law enforcement. I was very successful, and I now realize I was definitely guided. I always seemed to be in the right place at the right time. I was also a very good interviewer and knew exactly what questions to ask. They just came to mind, as though the person I was interviewing were telling me what to ask. I have lots of stories, funny and sad, I could share with you.

Just last year another "coincidence" guided me to the work of José Silva and his UltraMind ESP System, and I could see why my life turned out so well. More importantly, I realized that everyone who learns this simple system can have just as great a life, and even better.

Without any formal education, José Silva built a multimillion-dollar business, then he had great success as a scientific researcher. He also became a superb educator who seemed to know instinctively the right things to do.

The preconditioning modules in the Silva UltraMind ESP System are a brilliant method of leading the learner into the exercises. In training evaluation terms, they are the lesson plan for achieving the objectives of the learning, but are expressed in a dynamic method to match the whole ethos of the course. I am really impressed. The idea surely must have come from a higher source.

If you are reading this, I am sure that you, too, have been guided to it. Ask yourself: "Why did I choose this specific book of all the books on the shelf?"

When you follow the training process, and most importantly the key underlying principles, be ready for an amazing journey to the top.

Chris Downes, M.Ed., was a training evaluator and senior officer for the British police service from 1971 to 2001.

Preface

The Life of José Silva

José Silva's life is more than a great American success story. It has transcended time and space to become one of the world's all-time great success stories.

José Silva was born in Laredo, Texas in 1914. When he was just four years old, his father died as the result of a terrorist act during the Mexican revolution.

He started his first business at the age of six, when he began working and earning an income to help support the family—which included his sister and two younger brothers.

Since his income was necessary for the family, José never had the opportunity to attend school. With the help of his sister and brothers, he learned to read and write in both the Spanish and the English languages.

He recalled that he was always very lucky at finding new business ventures that would help more people and earn him more money.

He cleaned offices, ran errands, and eventually began traveling 150 miles to San Antonio to buy household goods that he then sold door-to-door in Laredo. By the time he was a teenager, he was employing other youngsters to go door-to-door and sell the merchandise. Many of the youngsters were earning more than their fathers, and young José was earning more than all of them.

That's how he had enough money to pay for a correspondence course in radio repair in 1928, when he was 14 years old. The timing was perfect. He got in on the ground floor of that new field, and that's how he earned his millions when he grew his electronics repair business to be one of the largest in South Texas.

He still had his knack for spotting new business opportunities. He recalled one time when he pointed out a vacant lot to his wife Paula and said it would be a great spot for an ice-cream stand. He didn't act on that impulse, because he had other interests, but a few months later somebody opened an ice-cream shop there.

José used his knowledge of electronics repair to start a new business repairing coin-operated music machines—juke boxes—and leasing them to establishments throughout South Texas.

In 1944, José was drafted into the army to serve during World War II. Not knowing whether he would survive the war, he closed his business and set the money aside for his family.

It was during the army induction process that José had his first encounter with a psychiatrist. This led him to the study of psychology. He dived into the study of psychology with the same enthusiasm he always had, because he wanted to see if he could learn ways to help his children to be as successful as he was. He had observed that only a few people had the kind of instincts and good luck that he had.

After his discharge from the army at the end of the war, José returned to Laredo and started his radio repair business all over again.

This was an exciting and busy time for him.

He was assigned to build a radio technician's training department at Laredo Junior College, and ran the department for more than six years. The department was named the best in the state of Texas by the Veterans Administration. This was quite an achievement for someone who had never attended school as a student.

When commercial television came on the scene, José began to learn all about it, and his business continued to grow rapidly.

His study of psychology had led him to several related fields, including hypnosis, parapsychology, and electroencephalography, leading to psychorientology, a new science of how to orient—or direct—your mind (psyche) for greater success.

After six years he was so busy with his business and his research that he had to resign his position at the college.

By 1966 the research has progressed so far that Silva was in demand to speak at colleges and universities about his work in psychorientology, and people throughout Texas were asking him to teach them his mind development techniques.

He had learned that the most successful people used their minds differently than the average person. Other people might work just as hard and have just as much knowledge, but if they didn't do their thinking at the alpha brain-wave level, then they weren't as successful as the 10 percent of people who did their thinking at that level.

The results of the research were tested at the University of Texas Medical Center and at Trinity University, both located in San Antonio. He showed the researchers that his students could do what scientists believed was impossible: activate the mind and function deductively while at the alpha brain-wave level.

The results were so impressive that they were published in a scientific journal in England in 1972. The scientists wanted to conduct more research with Mr. Silva, but school officials killed that idea when they learned that he didn't have any formal education.

He held no academic degrees, but received the kind of degree that you cannot get by taking tests in a classroom: the doctor of humanities degree for his life's work, which is the true test of greatness.

He always had great respect for education and wished he had been able to attend school, but someone once pointed out to him that every year, a lot of student parade across the stage and accept the Ph.D.'s they received for what they have learned, but only a few people receive an honorary doctorate for what they have actually accomplished.

He had the kind of education and experiences that no other scientist had.

His study of psychology taught him about human behavior.

His experiences with hypnosis showed him what the human mind is capable of doing.

The electroencephalograph (EEG) gave him the ability to see what was going on inside a person's head and relate brain activity to mental function.

In addition, he was a classically trained singer. His knowledge of music, frequencies, and harmonics revealed to him that scientists needed to rethink the way they had been classifying the brain-frequency spectrum.

Through the years he met many ultrasuccessful people. One of them was W. Clement Stone, author (with Napoleon Hill) of *Success through a Positive Mental Attitude*. It was more than just positive thoughts and mental images that enabled Stone to earn millions of dollars in the insurance business. "I could tell that Mr. Stone was also a natural alpha thinker, just like I am," Mr. Silva explained.

Positive thoughts and mental images of what you want to achieve have a small effect when you are functioning at the beta brain-wave level. But they have a very big impact when you are able to do your thinking at the alpha level.

Only one person in 10 learns naturally how to do their thinking at 10 cycles per second (cps), which is the alpha brain frequency. The good news is that José Silva developed a system to help everyone learn to function at 10 cps, just as the top 10 percent do.

He began teaching his system to the public in 1966, after spending half a million dollars of his own money to conduct 22 years of scientific research. In 1969 the demand for his services was so great that he began training other people to teach his system.

To date, millions of people in more than 100 countries around the world have benefitted from his research. He always offered a no-questions-asked money-back guarantee of satisfaction, and fewer than 1 percent ask for a refund.

The boy who was taught how to read and write by his siblings became a successful and sought-after author himself, authoring more than a dozen books. The first, *The Silva Mind Control Method*, published in English by Simon and Schuster, and eventually in more than a dozen other languages, has sold well over a million copies worldwide, and is still going strong 40 years after its first publication, making José Silva Laredo's most successful author.

The young boy who used to shine shoes for a living is the undisputed leader in the field of mind development and ESP. His system is the first to guide you to function at the alpha brain-wave level, to use the right brain hemisphere to think with, and to develop and use intuition (ESP).

Mr. Silva's philosophy has always been "to gain while helping others to gain, not to gain at others' loss."

This master of teaching people about success also cautions people to keep things in perspective: "Do not let the first failure destroy you, nor let success ruin you."

With the worldwide success of his system, Mr. Silva is known by more people around the world than anyone else who ever walked the streets of Laredo. He did not let success ruin him. He lived modestly, and his favorite pastime right up until his passing in 1999 was lecturing and helping other people awaken the genius that is within them.

This young boy, who started helping people one shoe at a time, went on to help millions, not just to look better on the outside, but to actually *be* better on the inside.

Prior to his passing he developed a new course, the Silva UltraMind ESP System. It is more than a course; it is a system.

In addition to helping people develop and use their own God-given intuition, the UltraMind ESP System includes a new scientifically based technique to communicate with higher intelligence regularly and reliably. This will enable you to obtain help and guidance in carrying out your mission in life.

While Mr. Silva may have moved on to new assignments, his work is still going strong, both in live seminars and in convenient home study courses.

José Silva is a glowing example of what people can achieve by using their natural, God-given intuition to make the right decisions and by concentrating on providing value to others, so that when they move on, they will have left behind a better world for those who follow.

Introduction

What This Book Is About

Businesspeople at all levels, from solo workers and entrepreneurs to department heads and top executives, require many skills.

Perhaps the most important is the ability to make good decisions in all aspects of creating and managing a profitable business.

Good decisions lead to company profits and career advancement.

The ability to sense people's inner thoughts and needs helps you say and do the right things to build a strong team that will quickly reach its goals and achieve great success.

Your intuition provides you with an additional source of information so that you will do the right thing at the right time and be ready when opportunities present themselves.

The good news is that now, thanks to the 22 years of scientific research by José Silva, we can help you succeed by teaching you how to use your natural, God-given intuition regularly and reliably so that you will be right more times than wrong.

Knowing the Future Helps You Prepare for It

When you know what the future holds, you will be prepared to deal with problems and take advantages of opportunities.

The benefits of this are obvious, but can it really be done?

Professor John Mihalasky, professor emeritus of industrial engineering at the Newark College of Engineering (now the New Jersey Institute of Technology), conducted 10 years of scientific research to find out.

In experiments he performed with company CEOs, he observed that the CEOs who performed best in tests of precognitive ability also tended to be the ones with the best success rates at running their business (measured in terms of five-year profitability growth).

Prof. Mihalasky's experiment results are summarized in the table below.

Percent profitability increase of the CEO's company over the previous five years	CEO precognition test score		
	Above Chance	Chance	Below Chance
Greater than 100%	81.5%	25%	27.3%
50% to 99%	18.5%	50%	18.2%
Below 50%	0%	25%	54.5%

Note that the CEOs with the greatest profitability increases (100% or more) also had the greatest number of correct guesses in intuition tests: 81.5% of them performed above chance results. On the other end, none of the CEOs with the poorest results scored above chance in the precognition test.

Of CEOs with mediocre numbers, the results were consistent with statistical chance results.

Professor Mihalasky will tell you more about what he learned in this project in appendix C. Even better, in this book we will guide you step-by-step to develop the ability to function the way the most successful executives do.

Successful People Attract Good Luck

Have you ever wondered why some people seem to make the correct decisions far more frequently than the average person?

It is because they use more of their mind, and use it in a special manner.

That is what you will learn to do in this book.

Early Adopters Reap the Benefits

Now is the perfect time for you to learn this new technology of the mind. With all new technology, the early adopters reap immediate benefits and gain big advantages before the establishment catches on and catches up.

It happened with the printing press, which made mass communications over great distances possible. People living in the American colonies exchanged information in booklets and newspapers and joined to create a new country.

It happened again with commercial television, when huge numbers of people could influence and be influenced by events and brought down a U.S. president and ended the Vietnam War.

We saw it happen just a few years ago in the Arab Spring, when the early adopters used the power of the Internet to change the way they are governed.

The computer, the Internet, and the smartphone have changed the way that all of us do business and communicate with one another.

Now humanity is poised to move beyond physical technology. We can use the human mind to go places where nothing else can go, to communicate in ways in which no other media in history have ever been able to communicate, and to solve insolvable problems and make impossible dreams come true.

We call it "the science of tomorrow—today," and those who adopt it first will benefit the most.

Who Will Benefit

Business owners, executives at all levels, managers, and supervisors will all learn valuable ways to use ESP to manage more effectively and make better decisions.

If you are an entrepreneur, an independent contractor, a home worker, an Internet marketer, or someone who sells goods on an online marketplace or auction site, you will benefit from enhanced creativity and decision making.

If you are looking for a new job, or if you desire to enter the business world, you will benefit from these techniques.

If you have struggled for years trying to rise above average and fulfill the potential you know you have, the answer is in your hands: unleash your superpowers by learning to use your mind the way the ultrasuccessful people do.

If you are part of a family business, we don't need to tell you about some of the special challenges you face. In addition to business relationships, you also have family relationships that can affect the success of the business.

Perhaps your job is managing a household and a family. That can be the toughest job of all. These techniques will help you to manage your family relations better and keep things running smoothly.

Testimonials and Case Studies

No matter what your age or where in the world you live, or how far along you are in your career, or whether you've had good fortune or bad, you can use your own natural, God-given intuition to help you in your business and personal life.

In chapter 1, business owner Klemen Mihelic in Slovenia explains how he used the Silva UltraMind techniques to help his family, his friends, and his business. He even came up with a solution to end the rape of women in refugee camps in Darfur, in the Sudan, that won praise from the humanitarian aid coordinator there.

A young man from Maryland, fresh out of college, used the Silva techniques to solve a difficult problem, and this one success helped get him out of a job that wasn't right for him and into the right career. You will meet him in chapter 2.

A California lady named Mona struggled for 23 years selling real estate with modest success. Soon after she start applying the techniques she learned in the Silva UltraMind ESP Systems, she doubled her results and quadrupled her confidence. She will tell you about it in chapter 5.

A retired executive who spent most of his career in the public sector in the United Kingdom discovered that it is much easier to make big-ticket spending decisions when you have reliable ESP in your tool kit. He explains what he did in chapter 6.

A lady in Bulgaria tells how she used subjective communication to get what she was rightfully entitled to despite the attempts of some unscrupulous people who tried to swindle her. You will learn what she did in chapter 9.

Entrepreneur Victor Kovens, who owns his own one-man travel agency, recounts how he obtained worldwide publicity and recognition as tops in his field for his business without hiring publicity agents or a public relations agency. You will meet him in chapter 11.

Ed Bernd Jr. will tell you, also in chapter 11, about negotiating his first publishing agreement with José Silva and how the words that he actually said to Mr. Silva were far superior than the words he had intended to say.

How to Develop Your Intuitive Powers

Now, thanks to the groundbreaking research by Mr. Silva, learning to use your own natural intuition is as easy as one, two, three:

1. Learn to function at the powerful alpha brain wave level with the relaxing, refreshing Silva Centering Exercise.
2. Unlock 100% of your intuitive powers with five simple mental projection drills.
3. Use your powers in ways that benefit both you and your customers.

Now, for the first time, we are going to open the vaults, go behind the scenes, and show you the science of how and why José Silva's world-famous mind training systems work. Better still, you will learn exactly how and when to apply this science in your own life and gain benefits you never imagined possible.

Would You Like to Learn How To . . .

Program yourself to do the right thing at the right time to take advantage of opportunities and increase profits and income?

Accurately forecast business trends to keep you ahead of the competition?

Use your intuition to help sense what other people's real wants and needs are?

Say the right thing at the right time when negotiating, managing subordinates, or reporting to superiors and shareholders?

Learn mental techniques to establish immediate rapport with co-workers, as well as with customers, clients, suppliers, and other people you deal with? (As long as you are being honest, you can create an instant connection with people so they know they can believe you and trust you.)

Use feedback in the physical world so that you know exactly what to do to achieve the success you desire?

Determine if the time is right to make a career move?

Detect industry trends before they become public?

Become aware of potential problems before they hurt you?

Program people who owe you money or who are trying to cheat you so that they develop a strong urge to do the right thing and pay you what they owe you?

Program your work environment for success?

Influence others from a distance even when you cannot be with them in person?

Mentally sense the right thing to say and do in order to produce the best outcome for your clients and your business?

Detect hidden information that will give you a competitive advantage by enabling you to serve your clients better?

Trust your judgment and your decisions, end doubt and second-guessing, by asking higher intelligence to confirm—or correct—your decisions?

Know when to seek a raise, a promotion, a better job?

Intuitively sense the true motivations and feelings of others and avoid the pain of being betrayed and disappointed?

Let higher intelligence guide you to your right path in life—for greater success, happiness, and satisfaction? Find your right work, your mission in life?

What You Must Do to Succeed

When you follow the simple step-by-step guidance in this book, you will find the powerful alpha brain-wave level. You will also learn to activate your mind while remaining at alpha in order to make better decisions and solve more problems. Just a few hours of relaxing and refreshing practice with José Silva's world famous Centering Exercise is all it takes.

Then relax at the alpha level and go through each of the five mental projection exercises to become familiar with the subjective (mental) dimension. You'll establish points of reference that you can use to solve problems and achieve positive outcomes that bring you success and satisfaction by improving living conditions on planet earth.

After that, you need to continue to use your learned techniques. Just a few minutes a day will keep you mentally sharp so that you will be a superior problem solver.

A word of caution: if you plan to use these abilities to take advantage of people, to gain benefits for yourself at their loss, then save your time and look elsewhere. Karma really works. The Creator does not favor one person over another, and will not help you if you want to gain at someone else's loss.

If you want to gain while helping the other person also gain, then these techniques will work for you, and higher intelligence will help you when you get stuck and need guidance and help.

Practical Techniques You Can Start Using Today

Your career. Do you want a better job? A raise? Something more meaningful, interesting, and satisfying to do? How about having your own business? More customers? Bigger sales? Better employees? Better working conditions?

Smart buying. Use remote viewing to find the best product or service, the best vendor to establish a relationship with. Then use remote influencing to help establish a relationship that will be mutually beneficial for years to come.

Effective selling. Would it help you to be able to mentally detect what your prospect's real wants and needs are—to read their thoughts, so to speak? Would it help you to be able to put a thought into your prospect's mind?

You can use remote viewing and remote influencing to reach them at a deep inner level, where they know you are telling them the truth, that what you are offering them really is in their best interest.

Neutralizing negativity in your prospect's mind; neutralize "negative generators" who are trying to sabotage the sale for their own selfish reasons.

Taking action. You can learn to use remote viewing to see what a person wants, and then use remote influencing to motivate them to go ahead and take action, to do what is right—to close the sale, to sign the agreement, to provide the information they've promised you, to pay a debt they owe you.

Earn Your Master's in Business Intuition

People spend a lot of money and a lot of time in class to earn an MBA: a master's degree in business administration.

Just as valuable—perhaps even more—is an MBI: master of business intuition.

The Silva UltraMind ESP System is like getting a degree in how to use intuition to detect information and solve problems.

In the first chapter of this book, you will start learning how to use more of your mind, and to use it in a special manner.

Claim Your Rewards

All forms of success—bonuses and raises and promotions and recognition and honors—come to those who are prepared and take action at the right moment in time.

In just a few weeks, you can equip yourself with the same skills and talents as the ultrasuccessful people in all walks of life, so that you can achieve the success that you have always known, deep within, that you are meant to have.

When you are ready to begin, just turn to chapter 1 and follow the simple instructions.

To contact us for help and support, please see the contact information in Appendix D.

Meet the Authors

José Silva Jr. was the first of José and Paula Silva's ten children. He was there when his father began the scientific research that unlocked the secret of developing intuition and using it regularly and reliably in all aspects of your life.

Nobody is more qualified than Joe Junior to teach you how to apply his father's research findings to your business career.

Joe was not a research subject. Joe documented the research, recording the sessions with an old Roberts reel-to-reel tape recorder, and filing the data that his father was acquiring.

While his younger sisters and brothers were sitting with their eyes closed, following their father's instructions, Joe was learning the best ways of helping the average person to develop mental powers that few people have.

When Mr. Silva realized that he needed to establish a business to propagate his findings, he called on Joe to help manage the new business, something Joe continues to do today. Twenty-five years later, when Mr. Silva started the new Silva UltraMind Systems business, at the age of 84, he put Joe in charge.

Katherine Sandusky came to work for José Silva in 1990, shortly after graduating from high school. She learned the business—and how to use the Silva techniques in business—from the ground up.

She started by taking orders, working in the mail room, and running the shipping department.

After a few years, she moved to Austin, Texas, and went to work in the state government bureaucracy.

While working for the state, she started her own Silva business, Avlis Productions Inc., and soon grew it into a full-time company, with representatives in many countries around the world. (By the way, if you are wondering where the name Avlis came from, just spell it backwards.)

In addition to managing the business, she is also a full-time mother to her young daughter, Lily.

Ed Bernd Jr. is another member of the Silva team. Ed grew up in the newspaper business. His motto was "Don't believe anything that you hear and only half of what you see." To say that he was cynical about the reality of ESP would be an understatement. "When I actually *experienced* it for myself, and could produce ESP repeatedly, then I couldn't deny it anymore," he admitted.

"When I realized how valuable this ability is for individuals and how much better life would be on this planet if everybody could use their intuition to get whatever they need without taking from anybody else, without hurting anyone, then I had to get involved.

When we reach that point, there will be no more need for crime, no more wars, and life will be good for everyone."

In 1977 Ed attended Silva instructor training to learn more, then began teaching the course. In 1981 he was offered at job at José Silva's Laredo headquarters. "I couldn't pass up an opportunity like that," he said, "and I have been here ever since," Ed recalls. "Joe was among the first to welcome me. 'Around here,' he told me, 'we don't think of you as an employee. We treat you like family.'"

Part One

How to Use More of Your Brain and Mind
the Way Ultrasuccessful People Do

1

A New Way of Living

Welcome to the beginning of the second phase of human evolution on the planet. Humans are beginning to use their minds in ways never imagined before.

In our highly connected world of mobile devices and social media and rapid change, it is essential that you not only keep up, but that you stay a step ahead of the competition.

If you are the first to know what is being planned before the plans are put into action, then you can be prepared for it. You will be able to stop bad things from happening and make good things happen.

Just as the personal computer, the Internet, social media, and the smartphone have revolutionized the way we communicate physically, you are now going to learn to use your mind to communicate *subjectively*. This will take you to places that you could never go before, and will allow you to communicate in ways that go beyond the wildest fantasies of science fiction.

This is now a reality, thanks to a scientific breakthrough that solved a mystery: what gives the ultrasuccessful people the ability to see what ordinary people don't see, and do what ordinary people don't do?

There are no limits to this new means of communication. Your mind is not physical, so physical barriers cannot stop it. If somebody is plotting against you, nothing can stop your mind from detecting it.

All it takes to access this new, unlimited means of communications is a computer that you already own. It is the most powerful computer in the world, a portable computer that you carry around in your head: your own brain.

Learning how to use this communications system is as easy as learning to use a smartphone: navigate to the application you need, then learn how to work with it.

In this book you will learn how to use your mind to detect information and solve problems.

You already know how to use your physical senses—such as eyesight and hearing—to detect information, and how to use your physical body to correct problems.

But 90 percent of us grew up without knowing how to use the mind that way.

Back in 1944, José Silva wanted to know more about how the brain and mind work so that he could help his children do better in school and be more successful in life. The research that he conducted over the next 22 years led to what has been called the greatest breakthrough of all time in the field of mind science.

How Your Brain Works

Your brain operates on a small amount of electricity, just like a computer. It can process and store information, retrieve that information, and use it to make decisions and solve problems.

The electrical energy of your brain pulsates, or vibrates, at various frequencies. Each frequency is associated with a specific part of your brain that is designed for a specific task:

1. Beta, more than 14 cps (typically 20), occurs when your body and mind are active and you focus your eyes.
2. Alpha, 7 to 14 cps, is associated with light sleep and dreaming.
3. Theta, from 4 to 7 cps, is associated with deeper sleep and with the use of hypnosis for such things as painless surgery.
4. Delta, below 4 cps, is associated with deepest sleep.

José Silva's professional background was in electronics, and this gave him insights that other researchers didn't have.

First, he reasoned that the best range to use for mental activity would be the range that has the least impedance and the most energy. Of the four frequencies, the alpha frequency has the strongest current and is the most rhythmic. That's why it was the first to be discovered by scientists in the 1920s using a sensing device called an *electroencephalograph* (EEG), which measures electrical energy in the brain. The scientists named this frequency *alpha* after the first letter in the Greek alphabet.

If it was actually possible to actively use one's mind to analyze problems and come up with solutions while in the alpha state, it seemed logical to José Silva that this state would be the ideal one in which to think. Why would the alpha level be ideal?

1. It would allow one to think more clearly because of its extra energy.
2. It would enable one to maintain concentration better.
3. Alpha is in the absolute center of the brain's normal operating range, so it would allow access to more information more easily.

But there was a catch. Research revealed that most people do their thinking at the beta frequency! José's research led him to discover that only 10 percent of the population are natural alpha thinkers. It turned out that he himself was one of them.

Most people, approximately 90 percent, are only able to use the weakest, least stable frequency to do their thinking: the beta level. Most people, when their brain frequency slows to alpha, enter the subconscious state, then fall asleep.

But the superstars stay awake at the alpha level, and do their thinking at alpha. These natural alpha thinkers have learned to use their intuition—to trust their hunches—and this guides them to far greater success than the average person.

The good news is that you have the same kind of biocomputer that they have. All that you need is instructions on how to access the alpha level, and then activate your subjective communication faculty with a few simple exercises to provide points of reference and orientate you.

José Silva had studied psychology and hypnosis while seeking ways to help his children. Once he obtained an EEG and actually saw how the brain functioned, he was able to combine his knowledge of all of those topics to develop a system that everybody can use to learn to function the way ultrasuccessful people do.

In this book, we will guide you step-by-step to activate and begin using your natural, God-given intuition like ultrasuccessful people—people like Klemen Mihelic, who owns a pre-press business in Slovenia.

Prospering during a Worldwide Recession

Do you remember the financial meltdown in late 2008 that led to a worldwide recession? Klemen Mihelic, who was just learning the Silva UltraMind ESP System, used his intuition so effectively that his business grew 90 percent in 2009, and has continued to grow ever since.

Klemen had taken the old Silva Mind Control course that was first introduced in the 1960s. It included many problem-solving techniques to help people overcome insomnia, relieve tension and migraine headaches, improve memory and concentration, stop smoking and overeating, and more.

Those techniques were included in order to attract people to class, so that they would then have an opportunity to learn the most valuable skill of all: developing and learning to use their own natural psychic abilities.

But there wasn't enough time left at the end of the course to teach people all the ways that ESP could help them in their business and personal lives, so most people thought the course was about the problem-solving formulas.

The course accomplished its main goal: millions of people in more than 100 countries around the world learned for themselves that ESP is real. Once people accepted the reality of ESP, José

Silva created the course he had always wanted to teach: the Silva UltraMind ESP System.

Klemen contacted us shortly after we launched the Silva Ultra-Mind ESP System and wanted to teach the course in Slovenia, where he lives. He'd had a lot of success with self-programming and with using the alpha brain-wave level to analyze business problems and select the best solution. He wanted to teach those techniques. But he told us that he didn't think the people of Slovenia were ready for an ESP course.

We disagreed, and explained some of the many ways that he could use ESP to help himself and his family in ways that went far beyond just relieving headaches and improving memory. He liked what he heard, so he agreed to give it a try and see what kind of results he got.

One of his first successes with the new techniques involved a problem he encountered about the construction of a new house. He used some alpha thinking and intuition to solve the problem.

"We had problems with our seller/investor who did not build the house as we both agreed at the beginning," Klemen explained. "There were too many mistakes."

First, he tried to correct the problem on his own by entering his level and picturing all of the mistakes corrected and the seller giving him some money to compensate him for the deficiencies.

"As I look back now," he said, "I realize that I really wanted too much money. So I went to level and told the seller, mentally, about mistakes and delays, and at my level he told me a few things that I had not considered. That is why I lowered my requests to him. At my level we both agreed with some corrections on the building, and we also agreed to a discount of $15,500.

"What happened the next day when I met the guy was amazing. He offered to correct exactly what I had programmed to be corrected, and he also offered me a discount of exactly $15,500. I was speechless!"

MentalVideo Solves Two Problems at Once

Following that, Klemen had a series of big successes with the help of the new MentalVideo technique (which you will learn in chapter 6). He was working on several unrelated problems.

He was expanding the building that housed his pre-press business, and needed somebody to oversee the construction work.

He was also trying to help a friend who had left a good job and taken another one that turned out to be a disaster. "When my friend told me his sad story, I started asking other friends for help. My beta plan was to find him some other job as soon as possible."

When Klemen was unable to come up with a solution to either problem, even with the help of alpha thinking and his own ESP, he turned to the MentalVideo to ask for help from higher intelligence.

The next day, a series of coincidences left Klemen in a jam, unable to find anybody who help him complete a simple task. Things seemed to be getting worse instead of better.

"As I was driving along," he said, "suddenly it came to me that I could hire my friend. As I thought about it, I realized that there was a lot of work he could do, including overseeing the construction work." His friend loved the idea, so Klemen hired him immediately. He also realized that once the construction was completed, his friend could do the graphic arts work that the printing company needed.

"Why did we fail to do the work so many times?" Klemen wondered. "As Mr. Silva said, all of those 'coincidences' let us know that higher intelligence was guiding us to a solution that many people would benefit from."

When the construction was completed, they began installation of a new state-of-the-art flexo plate making machine that they had ordered from Eastman Kodak Company. Nobody else in the area had this kind of capability, and they even had clients lined up from several neighboring countries.

"We fully started the production of flexo plates," he said. "We have bought very expensive new software to improve our quality. Kodak engineers were shocked when they saw our progress. We might be the first repro studio in the world with that kind of technology and knowledge, combined with the special software for flexo press.

"Actually they were now learning from us," Klemen continued, "and making notes. There is always some Kodak 'master' from Belgium, Great Britain, Israel, or other countries who want to come and see our progress. Strange? We are only a couple of Slovene enthusiasts, doing great work."

Then came the financial meltdown in October 2008 and the worldwide recession the following year. While most businesses suffered, and many shut down, Klemen used his new communications tools—ESP and the MentalVideo—to find opportunities where he and his customers would both benefit.

"We had enough customers," Klemen said, "but because of the financial crisis, payments were being delayed more and more because my customers were having trouble collecting money from *their* customers."

So he took it to the next level and began finding ways to use ESP, and help from higher intelligence, to help his customers' customers.

The result was a 90 percent growth in revenue in 2009, at the height of the recession.

An Inexpensive Solution to a Big Problem

Klemen had always worked to help people in need in Slovenia.

"What good is having money and the knowledge of how to get things done if you don't do some good with it?" Klemen asked. "Doing good is good business. The satisfaction that you get when you help somebody lets you know that you are a success."

Then in the fall of 2009, something else caught his attention: the refugee crisis in Darfur, in the western Sudan. He was especially troubled when he learned that women were being raped every night in the refugee camps because there were not enough people to police the area and protect them.

He used the MentalVideo to ask for a solution, and the next day he found it on the Internet: small, inexpensive, motion-activated, solar-powered video cameras.

Once the cameras were installed, the rapes were drastically reduced, because the perpetrators did not know when they were being recorded and feared they would be photographed and caught. The violence against the women ended immediately in a large area where the cameras were distributed.

Suleiman Jammous, humanitarian coordinator in Darfur, said in an interview, "I can tell you now that people in the refugee (camps) feel that Slovenia saved them more than EU and AU and the United Nations' 20,000 troops on the ground there.

"I think they are consuming money, millions and millions per day, and the effect they did was very minor to that effect made by these small cameras, sent from Slovenia, brought by my friend Tomo Kriznar and his colleague Klemen Mihelic," Suleiman continued.

"We didn't hear in the last two months about any kind of violations against women and children, thanks to these small cameras. They don't know where the camera is, and they are afraid to be caught, so everyone stopped. And this is known as the Slovenian gift."

Klemen wasn't looking to get any benefits for himself, but he got a huge unexpected benefit as a result of this work: he met a lot of interesting people and did a lot of great networking—United Nations and NGO officials, government leaders, CEOs, celebrities, and actors.

Now Klemen is working on even bigger plans: "We are now working to deliver the mobile drilling machines (mounted on trucks) for Darfurians to find water resources," he said. "We collected $200,000 to buy the machines, and we even persuaded Slovenian politicians to buy another one."

Actress Mia Farrow, who is a UNICEF Goodwill Ambassador, has offered to help Klemen's Humanitarian Organization for People around the Earth (HOPE) in the delivery of a drilling rig to Darfur. She explained, "There is nothing more human than giving people access to drinking water. This is worth dying for."

There was another crisis when Suleiman became critically ill and doctors thought that he would die. Klemen and his graduates in Slovenia programmed for Suleiman for almost a year, and he amazed the doctors by recovering to good health. "There are many, many more successes I could tell you about," Klemen said, "but we can save those for another time."

For more information about Klemen's work, please visit the HOPE website: www.hope.si.

Develop Your Own Subjective Communication Ability

Now that you have seen some of the value of intuition—and of using your intuition to request and receive guidance and help from higher intelligence—let's get started with the first step.

In the next chapter, you will learn how to find the alpha level and learn how to use it to solve problems and detect information.

How to Function Like a Genius

In this chapter you will learn to do something that only 10 percent of adults know how to do: use the most powerful part of your brain to think, analyze information, and create solutions to life's toughest problems.

In addition to being the most powerful part of the brain—where there is the least impedance to the flow of electrical energy and therefore of thoughts—it is also the area that some psychologists have labeled the *subconscious*. You are now going to learn how to use the subconscious consciously.

How José Silva Discovered the Alpha Level

José Silva's field was electronics, so when he learned about a machine called the EEG, which could actually measure the electrical energy coming from the brain, he bought one.

He might have been the only person in the world who was an expert in both hypnosis and electronics. This gave him the insight and ability to investigate what was happening to the brain physically while it was engaged in various mental activities, and to understand what was going on.

He had also studied psychology, which gave him insight into human behavior. His study of music contributed too by helping him to understand frequencies and harmonics. It enabled him to comprehend the relationships of the various frequencies that come from different parts of the brain.

Mr. Silva used to bring people into his laboratory, connect them to the EEG, and ask them questions. Most of the time, the people's brain frequency would remain at 20 cycles per second beta the whole time, but in some people—about one in 10—their brain frequency would lower to 10 cycles alpha while they thought about the question, and would then come back to 20 cycles beta when they answered him.

He noticed that these people were more successful, healthier, and luckier than the 90 percent who remained at beta when they did their thinking.

This made sense to him from an electronics point of view. If the alpha level is the strongest, he reasoned, that means it has the least impedance to the flow of electrical current. It is the most efficient circuit in the brain. At alpha, there are the fewest impediments to clear thinking. Therefore it is the ideal frequency to use for thinking.

Subsequent research bore out this hypothesis. He would bring children into the laboratory—it is very easy to take children to the alpha level—and he would ask them questions. He might ask them how many ways they could think of to clean a car, for instance. They would tell him everything they could think of: wash it, vacuum it out. Then he would take them to alpha and ask them again, and they would come up with additional ideas: polish the hubcaps, clean the windows and the windshield wipers, and so on.

These findings indicated that there is more information available to us at alpha than there is at beta. This could partly explain why the 10 percent of humanity who are alpha thinkers are more successful than those who do their thinking at beta.

All of the ultrasuccessful people are natural alpha thinkers. They have learned, through some natural means, to do their thinking at alpha. But they don't realize that they think differently than 90 percent of humanity. When they write their books telling people how to achieve great success, only 10 percent of their readers can use those techniques successfully, because they are the only ones who do their thinking at the alpha level.

That is why those authors can always point to a few people who use their techniques successfully, while most of their readers get little benefit. Many "self-improvement" courses work the same way: the natural alpha thinkers are trying to teach their techniques to people who are unable to do their thinking at the alpha level.

All of our techniques are designed to function at the alpha level. That is why it is so important to practice the Silva Centering Exercise (Long Relaxation Exercise) from time to time to maintain a good, deep alpha level. (For instructions, see appendix A.) You need to use it enough in the beginning so that you can relax physically and mentally and remain relaxed while you do your programming. Practice it at least three times. Mr. Silva recommended accumulating 10 hours of practice at your level to ensure that you have established a deep, healthy level of mind to function from.

In fact, Mr. Silva said this was his greatest discovery: a way to use the subconscious consciously, thus converting it to an "inner conscious level." There are many benefits from being able to do this.

Benefits of Alpha Thinking

Just like the alpha brain wave frequency, the alpha part of the brain is centrally located, and therefore it is closer to the information that has been impressed and stored on your brain neurons.

When your mind is functioning at the alpha brain-wave level, it has access to more information, it can process more information and process it faster, and it can find solutions faster than is possible at the beta level.

This makes alpha the ideal level for analysis and complex decision making. The beta level is for action. If you've been having trouble making good decisions, now you know why: you have been doing it at beta, the weakest, least stable, least synchronous part of the brain.

Alpha also gives you access to subjective—mental—information. You can detect information with your mind—your psyche—that is not available to your physical senses. This access to psychic information gives natural alpha thinkers a big advantage over ordinary people.

Imagine using a part of your brain and mind that you have probably never used consciously in order to obtain information from other people's brains, and to use their information—and their experiences—as if they were your own.

Think about what that means. When you can access other people's experiences and results, you can learn from their experiences. You can learn from their mistakes and learn what worked well for them, so that you can avoid making the same mistakes and can do it right the first time.

There is still more: imagine receiving information and guidance and help from a higher power. We call it *higher intelligence*.

Other people call it God or Allah or Jehovah or the Almighty or many other names. This higher intelligence is vast enough and great enough to help everyone who is solving problems and making the world a better place to live.

Imagine presenting your proposal, and knowing that this higher power is working through you to help persuade people to follow your lead.

More Benefits of Using the Alpha Level

There are many more benefits of learning to use the subconscious consciously:

- The alpha level leads to better health by strengthening your immune system, so it is like having free health insurance—the kind that protects you from developing health problems.
- It is the strongest part of the brain, with the most synchronous and most stable brain frequency, so you can do a better job of analyzing information and making decisions.
- You will be safer from accidents, because your mind will automatically use ESP to detect oncoming danger and automatically guide you to the right action to avoid it. (You will learn how to develop your ESP in chapter 3.)
- You will be luckier, because your ESP will automatically make you aware of opportunities that 90 percent of people won't know about because they haven't learned to use the subconscious consciously.
- You will be more persuasive, because your mind will communicate directly with the people you are trying to persuade.

- You will be fresher and more alert. Fifteen minutes of time at alpha give you as much benefit as one hour of sleep. Look at what that means for the bottom line: invest 20 minutes at alpha and gain an additional 40 minutes of time to work or play or whatever you like. That is a pretty good return on investment, isn't it?

- You can also use the alpha level to help you overcome bad habits, like drinking too much or drug addiction. You can also use the alpha level to start beneficial new habits that will help you achieve the business success you desire.

- Alpha is the level for creativity. But you say you are a manager, not a creative person, so why do you need to develop your creative side? Here's why: when the solutions you are using aren't producing the results you need, you need new solutions. That's where your creative side comes in: the creative alpha level. Need more revenue? Use the alpha level to help you find a new service or product. Problems with an employee? Use the alpha level. Problems obtaining the materials you need at a price that will allow you to make a profit? Then head to alpha for creative solutions.

- Alpha will help you to balance work and family in the midst of demanding job requirements. All work and no play can be bad for your health and productivity, so at alpha you might realize that you will benefit by learning to play better golf or improve your skill at any other activity. Research has shown that practicing a skill mentally at the alpha level brings almost as much improvement as practicing physically.

- You can also use this inner conscious level to go back in time—subjectively—and rewrite your personal history. If you had bad experiences that affected your belief in your ability to achieve greatness, you can neutralize those beliefs by impressing new ones at the same level, in the same part of the brain where those old childhood beliefs are stored.

The first step is to find the alpha level and learn to function there with conscious awareness. This will allow you to use the subconscious consciously. In other words, you convert the subconscious into the inner conscious level.

It All Begins with Alpha

First, you will learn to function at the alpha level with your eyes closed, because any time you attempt to use your physical eyesight, your brain will adjust to the beta brain wave frequency.

Later, in chapter 8, we will teach you how to function with your eyes open and still get the full benefits of alpha functioning.

First, though, we want you to learn to function at the alpha level with your eyes closed and verify that you are doing it.

As a businessperson, you know how important it is to evaluate results and measure their impact on the bottom line. This is what leads to recognition, raises, bonuses, and promotions to higher and more responsible positions.

It is easy to measure the results you achieve by using the alpha level. When you are able to solve problems that you couldn't solve at the beta level, then you know you are getting a good return on your investment.

That is exactly what happened to a Silva graduate in Maryland. Here is his story:

Stubborn Problem Yields Quickly to Alpha Thinking

L.J. of Maryland discovered the power of alpha thinking shortly after starting his first job. "I was right out of college," he recalled. "I had taken the first engineering job that I could find. It involved troubleshooting control boards for a missile control system."

He wasn't sure that he wanted to do this kind of work, and he didn't seem to be very well suited to it.

"One day, a board came my way, and for the longest time, I could not figure out what was wrong with it," he said. "I gave it my best shot. My emotions raised when I started to realize that this was not my calling."

Then he remembered his Silva training and decided to see if he could use the power of the alpha level to find the problem. "I managed to relax enough to get to the alpha level, and let the answer come to me as a mental picture."

He used mental pictures to compare the circuit the way it was to the way it should be, and he noticed that one area stood out. "I came out of level, used my volt meter (ohm meter), and indeed the problem was there."

That success had far-reaching consequences for L.J. "This experience not only helped me keep my job, but led me to realize that I needed to find another position, which I did within the same company. I even ended up disclosing a patent in the new job!"

L.J. benefitted. So did his employer, and so did the person who was hired to fill the job that L.J. didn't like after he moved into his new position with the company.

Several Ways to Learn the UltraMind ESP System

I am going to give you four ways to learn our system without attending a class:

- Use daily countdown deepening exercises.
- Memorize the Silva Centering Exercise to practice on your own.
- Record the Silva Centering Exercise.
- Have someone read the Silva Centering Exercise to you. You can team up with a partner and help each other learn.

If you use a recording of the Silva Centering Exercise, please be sure to use one with José Silva's original wording—his original phrases—not one of the modified versions that were changed by somebody else after his passing. The original Silva Basic Lecture Series or his UltraMind ESP System will have the original version.

Relaxation Leads to Alpha

The Silva system is not book learning. It is subjective experiencing. It is just like learning any other skill: you must practice to develop expertise and gain the confidence that will let you excel.

When you become passive and relaxed physically and mentally, your brain frequency slows down. This happens when you go to sleep at night. It happens when you are relaxed and daydreaming. But if you haven't learned to stay at alpha when you activate your mind, then your brain frequency will increase whenever you become mentally or physically active.

After you learn to enter the alpha level, then you can learn to activate your mind and *remain* at the alpha level by practicing a series of "mental calisthenics" that José Silva developed during his 22 years of scientific research. He was the first scientist to discover how to do this, and his groundbreaking research was published in the medical journal *Neuropsychology* in 1972.

The fastest and easiest way to learn is to have someone guide you to relax, and then to practice the mental calisthenics. There are several ways to do this without attending a live seminar:

You can go to the website www.SilvaNow.com and stream or download a recording of the Silva Centering Exercise.

There is another way to practice that can save time: you can be your own lecturer by recording the Silva Centering Exercises and the other conditioning cycles.

You can talk to a recording device as if it were you. You can give yourself instructions to close your eyes and take a deep breath. You can instruct yourself to relax all the parts of your body. You can tell yourself to picture tranquil and passive scenes to induce a relaxed mind.

To get started now, there is a complete script of the Silva Centering Exercise in appendix A in the back of this book. You can follow the instructions and make your own recording, in your own voice. Or you can ask someone else to record it for you.

If you are learning the Silva system along with someone else, you can take turns reading it to teach other. They can watch you and pace themselves depending on how quickly you relax, and you can do the same for them.

If none of these approaches are practical for you, then you can go to appendix A and follow the instructions there to memorize the basic steps that we use in the Silva Centering Exercise, then close your eyes and do it for yourself. José Silva's brother Juan always believed that it is better to do it yourself than to have somebody else guiding you.

If you find yourself making an effort to recall the instructions, and therefore are not relaxing completely, then you can use the Morning Countdown system in appendix B.

José Silva recommended that when you learn on your own, you should accumulate a total of 10 hours of practice with the Silva Centering Exercise in order to be confident of your ability to function at the alpha level.

All of our techniques are designed to work at the alpha level. However, once you learn, you will not need to go through the Centering Exercise to get to alpha. You won't even need to close your eyes. You will be able to have alpha functioning with your eyes open as long as you don't focus and concentrate your eyesight on anything. We'll explain that a little later in this book.

Do Not Skip Any Steps

The first time you take this training, please be sure to do everything in the order that we present it.

First, you need to establish the alpha level. Practice the Silva Centering Exercise at least three times.

Then there are five mental projection exercises that are the key to learning this new "subjective" communications system. Please do them in the order that we present them, because each one builds on what you learned in the previous ones.

In the live seminars, we do the Silva Centering Exercise before each of the mental projection conditioning cycles. It will be best if you do the same. Here is the order.

___ Silva Centering Exercise

___ Projection to Home

___ Silva Centering Exercise

___ Projection into Inanimate Matter Kingdom

___ Silva Centering Exercise

___ Projection into Plant Life Kingdom

___ Silva Centering Exercise

___ Projection into Animate Matter Kingdom

___ Silva Centering Exercise

___ Projection into Human Kingdom

After you have completed the training, then you can maintain your ability by using what you have learned to solve problems. We recommend that you go to the alpha level at least once a day, for five minutes. Twice a day is better; three times a day is excellent.

To practice for five minutes each time is good; 10 minutes is better; 15 minutes is excellent.

Now when you are ready to begin, choose the method that is best for you. Either use the recording on the www.SilvaNow.com website, or go to appendix A or B and follow the instructions.

3

Decision-Making Techniques

In the next five chapters you will practice the five mental projection exercises that will introduce you to the subjective dimension. Meanwhile, please continue to practice your alpha exercise as we instructed you to in chapter 2 to make sure that you will be at the alpha level when you practice the mental projection exercises.

When you feel relaxed physically and mentally, you are doing it correctly. When you feel relaxed and energized at the completion of your alpha exercises, you know you are entering the alpha level.

You cannot "feel" alpha, but relaxation creates the environment where your brain will produce the alpha brain wave that we desire.

To help you learn to actually use the alpha level, I will give you some techniques that you can use at alpha to help you in your business career as well as in your personal life. You can use these techniques immediately, even while you are doing the five mental projection drills to develop your ESP.

It is easy to measure the results you achieve by using the alpha level: you take action and notice the results that you get.

José Silva often emphasized the importance of taking action. The whole course is based on taking action. That is why we urge students in class not to just sit passively as their instructor reads the conditioning cycle to them, but to actually follow the instructions and do what the instructor tells them to do.

That is why doing it on your own can be more valuable to you. As a businessperson, you recognize—just as José Silva did—the importance of actually doing what is necessary to ensure that you get the results you want.

You can remain relaxed so that you stay in the alpha level. Also follow the simple instructions about how to use your mind.

Correct Attitude

Successful businesses provide products and services that have value to people. Henry Ford put a car in every garage, Bill Gates helped find a way to put a computer in every home, Steve Jobs took it even further and put a computer in everybody's hand.

As consumers, we are happy to give money to people who provide us with benefits and advantages that we desire.

This concept extends beyond life here on planet earth. If you want to obtain guidance and help from higher intelligence, which you will learn to do in chapter 6, you need to do what higher intelligence sent us here to do, which is to solve problems and improve living conditions here on earth.

It turns out that the Golden Rule is good business. To help us do our best, José Silva created the Laws of Programming.

The Laws of Programming

Before I give you the specific problem-solving techniques that you can use at the powerful alpha level, I need to advise you that this level is not to be used to cheat other people and take advantage of them. José Silva always told us that we should not gain at somebody else's loss. We should gain while helping the other person to also gain.

To guide us in doing that, he included five Laws of Programming in the UltraMind ESP System. Laws are fixed, laid down; they are not optional. Laws don't break. If you jump off the roof, the law of gravity won't break—but you will.

If you are not achieving the success you feel you should be achieving, then review the Laws of Programming and make sure you are complying with them. Here they are:

- Do to others only what you like to have others do to you.
- The solution must help to make this planet a better place to live.
- The solution must be the best for everybody concerned.
- The solution must help at least two or more persons.
- The solution must be within the area of possibility.

Klemen Mihelic, the business owner you met in chapter 1, had this to say about the value of the Laws of Programming in an email he sent to us in January 2008:

> Do you remember when you told me I am not the only one who is programming for more business? Most businesses want more business, but not all of them pay as much attention to whether they are giving their customers as much value as possible.

Ever since you told me that, I have kept in my mind the five Laws of Programming, and I must tell you that the Laws of Programming are all you need in the beta world.

From the time I took the old course many years ago, I have programmed a lot to successfully run my business, but nothing works better than the five Laws of Programming. I am so happy that José Silva decided to include them in the UltraMind ESP System. Be honest and do good for others and you will profit! It simply works!

More Information at Alpha

As you now know, the 10 cps alpha frequency is at the center of the normal brain wave frequency range, which runs from 0.5 cps delta to 20 cps beta. It is located at the midbrain area, the center of the brain. The center is the ideal place to be in order to access as much information as possible from all parts of the brain.

That is one reason that the alpha level is the ideal level for analyzing problems and using your lifetime of experience to find the best solution. Here is an example from our own business:

One of our affiliates had built a website to sell the Silva Ultra-Mind ESP System Complete Home Seminar. Sales were good, but we were getting too many returns. We entered the alpha level and mentally scanned the website and immediately were attracted to the main headline:

Develop ESP in two days, guaranteed . . . or your money back.

We had been using that headline very successfully for our two-day seminars, and that was where the affiliate had seen it.

It was fine for a two-day seminar, but not so good for a home study course. Very few people will sit down and listen to 17 hours of recordings in two days. One of the advantages of the Home Seminar is that you can take it at your convenience, at your own pace.

We suggested that he change the headline to read:

Develop ESP in as little as two weeks, guaranteed . . . or your money back.

Once we changed the headline to give people a more realistic idea of how long it would take to get results, returns dropped dramatically.

This truly conforms to the Laws of Programming. It was the best thing for everybody concerned. More people learned and benefitted from the UltraMind ESP System, they learned techniques to help their loved ones and anyone who needed help, and we made more sales and earned more money.

It is a false choice to think that when one person gains, somebody else has to lose. José Silva said that we should gain while helping the other person to gain as well.

You can use your mind to detect where the objective reality fails to conform to the subjective blueprint of perfection, so that you can then correct the abnormality and everybody gains

Help for Decision Making

Your success in business may be determined by the decisions you make. Your judgment is being tested. This is not the first time. You have made many good decisions. You have been right more often than wrong in the past, and that is probably why you are where you are in your business career.

Now you have ways to use more of your mind, more of your decision-making capability, more of your latent genius ability, to be right even more often.

There is more information available at alpha than at beta, and alpha is the strongest part of the brain, so it is the ideal level to use to analyze problems and decide how to correct them.

In addition to that, here are a couple of very powerful decision-making techniques.

- You can use José Silva's Elimination Technique (below) to help you make the right choice when you have several options.
- You can use Silva UltraMind's MentalVideo technique, which you will learn in chapter 6, to help you choose the best option, and also to give you guidance when you don't know what to do next.

The Elimination Technique

With the Elimination technique (also called the Alternate Choice technique), you compare two of the available choices at a time. It is much like a single-elimination sports tournament, where teams play each other and the loser is eliminated, while the winner moves on.

Let's say you have an opportunity to make a sizable sale to a new company. You have three star salespeople to choose from. You must select the one best for this critical sale. You review the matter objectively.

Then you go to your center, the alpha level. At your center, you pose the question: who is better, salesperson A or salesperson B?

Then clear your mind for a moment by thinking of something entirely different. You want to disconnect from the "asking" mode and reconnect in the "receiving" mode. When you return to the question to get the answer, your first impression is usually the strongest, and the correct one.

After you have eliminated one of the two choices, compare the one you chose with another option. If you feel that salesperson A is the better one for the job, then your next step is to compare salesperson A with salesperson C. Once again, choose one and eliminate the other.

You can use this method for small decisions at first. See how clairvoyant decisions work for you in using this person instead of that person, in using this color instead of that color, this equipment instead of that equipment. As your skill improves, and your confidence grows, you can graduate to the important situations that can bring you big savings in time.

For instance, you can be doing some routine tasks where a certain amount of good judgment is needed. You have done these tasks satisfactorily many times before the Silva training. But now, with the Silva techniques, you can do them even better. You can use the elimination method at alpha in:

- Pricing products
- Setting manufacturing runs
- Determining discounts to be allowed
- Evaluating credit limits
- Establishing budgets
- Hiring the best employees
- Ordering raw materials
- Establishing inventory levels
- Effective advertising and marketing
- Negotiating
- Crisis management

The result will be a fine-tuning of your judgment. Routine matters, instead of being handled in a routine way, will enjoy the same superior touch as more important matters. Furthermore, routine matters occur more frequently. So the small increment of advantage you gain adds up rapidly. You begin to see it in the profit-and-loss statement.

This technique can yield:

- Better words and phrases in a letter or ad
- The proper order of procedure in written material or activities
- The diplomatic approach in conversation
- The right area for a sales test
- The best person to do a job

Suppose you are comparing two suppliers, one who offers compensation if you have less than 99 percent uptime, versus another supplier who guarantees 98 percent uptime. Would you pay 50 percent more to gain an extra 1 percent uptime? It doesn't sound like a very good deal from a left-brain perspective.

Doing your analysis at alpha, you might look at it from another angle and realize that you will have twice as much downtime before receiving compensation if you opt for the 98 percent uptime guarantee. Compare prices on that basis, and you may decide that paying 50 percent more for a guarantee of 100 percent more uptime might be the better deal.

There are many other situations where the alpha level can help you make the best decisions.

You are making a major purchase and several suppliers are competing. Compare them on these bases:

- Innovative new company versus trusted established company
- Lower purchase price versus lower price for service contract
- Cost of additional features versus savings in increased productivity
- Hiring the best employees
- Establishing budgets
- Ordering raw materials
- Setting manufacturing runs
- Establishing inventory levels
- Setting prices
- Determining discounts to be allowed
- Evaluating credit limits
- Effective advertising and marketing
- Negotiating
- Crisis management

Chris Downes, a retired British police officer (who wrote the foreword to this book), used the Alternate Choice technique to make an important buying decision in his personal life.

I was buying a new car and I had narrowed it down to one of two choices. I came up with my own variation of the Alternate Choice technique. I visualized both cars, and imagined them both being driven inside a garage and the door closing.

Then I cleared my mind by thinking of something else I needed to do, and when I came back for the answer, I imagined the garage door opening and one of the cars coming out. But I didn't call and order it right away.

Within 30 minutes, one of the car dealerships telephoned me to say there was a problem on the construction line and the car would not be available until sometime in September. That confirmed what the technique had indicated about which one to buy.

I am sure it helps that I have been practicing the distant healing that we learn in the last part of the Silva UltraMind ESP System, and also using the MentalVideo [see chapter 6] for guidance from higher intelligence.

How to Develop Your ESP and Use It Reliably

These days it seems as if there are apps for everything.

Tap a button or an icon, and somebody will bring you a pizza, or give you a ride, or play your favorite music, or show you the latest movie, or even read a book to you.

But there are some things that only a human being can do. Only a human being can fall in love; a computer app can't do it for you.

Intuition is also something that only a living being can do.

For centuries, people have tried to understand and explain ESP—psychic ability. Some people thought it was some kind of mysterious "extra sense" that only a few lucky people had. That's why they called it *extrasensory perception*. In a way, they were right, because, as we have seen, only a few lucky people—about 10 percent of humanity—have learned how to use this ability.

There were many other ideas about psychic ability. José Silva sorted through all of them during his 22 years of scientific research. He put all of them to the test. He discovered that ESP is not an *extra* sense but a *prior* sense—something we are all born with but which only one person in 10 is able to use after they mature.

Mr. Silva's greatest discovery is how easy it is for all of us—everybody—to develop this ability. He discovered that it is not something extra, and we don't have to sit and hope that it comes to us. That is why he changed the meaning of ESP to *Effective Sensory Projection.* You can project your mind to detect any information anywhere it exists.

We are going to do something now that we have never done before.

We will open the vault and show you exactly what José Silva discovered about how to develop your own natural, God-given intuition within one week or less.

You have already learned the first step: how to enter and function at the alpha brain-wave level.

Now I will show you the second step: how to learn to decode and understand the subjective (mental or psychic) information, just as your smartphone decodes digital information.

How Psychic Ability Works

Effective Sensory Projection is a lot like your smartphone. When we talk on the phone, you hear my voice, and I hear your voice.

But you don't hear my actual voice, and I don't hear your actual voice. My phone converts my voice into computer code and then transmits it through an electronic signal to your phone.

Your phone decodes the data sent to it by my phone and converts it back into sound waves that resemble my voice.

We each hear a representation of the other person's voice created by our phone from the information that the other phone sent.

The same thing happens when you use video messaging. What you see on your screen is an image of the person that your smartphone reconstructed from the digital code that was sent from their phone. You see a reproduction of my face that is created by the app on your phone, and I see a likeness of your face that the app on my phone creates.

ESP works the same way: your mind detects psychic information, and apps in your brain will decode the information and convert it to a physical representation.

Your brain's clairvoyant app will give you a mental picture, your clairaudient app will provide a reproduction of sounds, and your clairsentient app affects your physical body directly.

Nobody else is doing it. Your mind detects the subjective (psychic) information, and your brain decodes it and converts it to a form that you can understand.

But there is one big difference between a smartphone and your brain:

Using your smartphone to communicate and send information back and forth requires that both parties participate.

Not so with your mind. You can project your mind to any location and detect information if it is needed to solve a problem and improve living conditions on the planet.

If another person is at the alpha level and is projecting a mental image to you, then it is easy for you to detect it while at your alpha level.

If they are not projecting a mental image to you, then you may need to create an image with your own mind. It might not happen automatically. You might have to take action mentally and create a mental image, or perhaps several mental images, until you find the correct one.

You can also imagine what someone would say to you, and what they might feel like. This is how you can detect accurate information when nobody is transmitting it to you.

Take the First Step to Develop Your ESP

Now we will take the first step in developing your own natural God-given intuition, which you can do in just a few days' time.

In order for you to become familiar with the subjective (mental) dimension, we want you to enter the alpha level and go over what you already know, what you have experienced, to review what you have impressed on your brain neurons with your objective (physical) senses.

What are you already familiar with in your everyday life? You are familiar with your own home. When you walk into a room, you know immediately which room it is and how it is furnished, because you have been here before. There are many distinguishing details that you can refer to so that you know whether you are in the living room or the dining room or the master bedroom. These details are called *points of reference.*

Points of Reference

Points of reference are details that help you to recognize and understand something. That is what you do whenever you learn something new, like learning to read a balance sheet.

In order to recognize and understand a balance sheet, you

first need to know what assets, liabilities, and equity accounts are. Then, when you see them laid out a certain way, you will know that you are looking at a balance sheet. The more experience you have with balance sheets, the faster you will be able to use one to determine the financial health of a business.

A balance sheet lays out the ending balances in a company's asset, liability, and equity accounts as of the date stated on the report. The most common use of the balance sheet is as the basis for ratio analysis, to determine the liquidity of a business. Liquidity is essentially the ability to pay one's debts in a timely manner.

The balance sheet is a key element in the financial statements; other documents are the income statement and the statement of cash flows. A statement of retained earnings may sometimes be attached.

The format of the balance sheet is not mandated by accounting standards, but rather by customary usage. The two most common formats are the vertical balance sheet (where all line items are presented down the left side of the page) and the horizontal balance sheet (where asset line items are listed down the first column, and liabilities and equity line items are listed in a later column). The vertical format is easier to use when information is being presented for multiple periods.

All of these details can be seen as points of reference for understanding a balance sheet. In order to learn to function in the subjective dimension just as easily as you function now in the objective, physical dimension, you need to start collecting experiences and finding distinguishing details in the subjective dimension that you can refer to.

Here is what José Silva discovered about how to do that:

Beginning to Explore the Subjective Dimension

First, we will take your objective experiences to the subjective—alpha—level and will review them at that level. We will go over and review the experiences and memories that you have accumulated in your brain.

Then we will ask you to do something with your mind that you cannot do with your body. In this way, you will establish subjective impressions with your mind. You can do that when you are at 10 cycles per second alpha. We will call this *mental projection*.

For instance, you know what your living room looks like physically, so in order to experience it mentally, you will project your mind into the material that the wall is made of. You cannot do this physically, so you must use your mind and do it mentally.

The following is what we want you to do in order to begin to familiarize yourself with the subjective dimension, so that you will be able to use your ESP and function as a psychic.

As you did before, you can memorize the following, or record it and play it back while you are at the alpha level, or have someone read it to you. Allow enough time to do each of the things you are instructed to do.

This is a long exercise, so if you do it on your own, you can begin with just the first section. Then you can add the second section and do both the first and second sections. Then add the third section the next time.

It is fine to go back and review anything you have already learned, but please don't skip ahead. Everything we do builds from one step to the next, so please do everything in order the first time.

Remember: if you record these instructions and listen to the recording, or if you have someone read them to you, then you can do the entire exercise—all four segments—in one session.

If you are memorizing what to do and then doing it on your own without anybody guiding you, then it will be easier to do it one segment at a time.

Give It Time to Work

After you do these mental projection drills at your center—the alpha level—it is important for you to give them time to work. After you come out of your level, do something else, and let your experiences settle in.

If you work with a partner who reads the exercise to you, do not talk about your experiences afterward until you've had a chance to "sleep on it."

Mr. Silva said it is like planting a seed: you need to give it time to sprout; you can't dig it up to look at it right away.

Once you have gone through at least one sleep and dream cycle—about 90 minutes of sleep—then it is OK to talk about it if you feel there is a need to.

Now when you are ready, here is what we want you to do:

Projection to Home

Project yourself mentally to be standing in front of your home, standing about 30 feet (10 meters) from it. Look at your home. You have been here many times.

Begin scanning the scene at the upper left-hand corner, going slowly from left to right, as you do when reading a book, going lower each time until you reach the ground level. (pause)

Study colors as you do this. What color is the roof? (pause) If there is a tree in front of your house, what color is the tree? (pause) Study details. Recall what you have seen. Remember it. Remembering what you have seen is called *visualizing*. (pause)

Allow yourself enough time to do this; then, when you reach the ground level, focus your attention on the front door and concentrate on the doorknob or handle. (pause) Mentally move close to the door, close enough to touch the door handle; expect the door to appear to increase in size as you get closer. (pause) Mentally touch the doorknob or handle; open the door; mentally enter your home, closing the door behind you. (pause)

Mentally walk toward your living room. Once you have entered your living room, stand at the center, facing the south wall. (pause) You have been here before; you have been here during daylight hours; you have been here during nighttime, with the lights turned on, and with the lights turned off.

It is now daytime; you are standing at the center of your living room facing the south wall. You have been here before, you know how much light enters this room during the day, and you recognize what is in front of you; (pause) what is behind you. (pause) You know what is to your left (pause) and what is to your right. (pause)

Now we will change the scene to nighttime with the house lights turned on. The scene has changed to nighttime, and you are still standing in the middle of the living room, facing the south wall. You have been here before, and you know what is in front of you, (pause) what is behind you, (pause) what is to your left, (pause) and what is to your right. (pause)

Now the lights will go out. The lights are out, and you are standing in darkness facing the south wall. Although the living room looks dark, you still know what is in front of you, (pause) what is behind you, (pause) what is to your left, (pause) and what is to your right. (pause)

At this time concentrate on the wall before you, the south wall. You can sense it being a certain distance away, and you know what is on this wall; you also know the color of this wall. Use your memory, your knowing, your sensing, to make a study of your south wall.

Scan this wall as you did the front of your home, beginning at the upper left corner and going from left to right, a little lower each time until you reach the floor level. Study everything that attracts you: pictures, curtains, and furniture. Especially concentrate on objects that contain color. Give yourself enough time to do this. (pause)

You have practiced entering deep, healthy levels of mind. In your next session, you will enter a deeper, healthier level of mind, faster and easier than this time.

Now when you are ready, count yourself out of your level. Take your time.

Time in the Subjective Dimension

If you are wondering why we use the south wall, it is because when we face south mentally, we can move forwards and backwards in time. It doesn't matter which way you face physically. It is as if you have moved out of the physical dimension into the mental dimension, and now you are looking back (mentally) at the physical dimension.

In the physical dimension, the past is behind you, the present is where you are, and the future is in front of you.

In the mental dimension, the past is to your right, the present is directly in front of you, and the future is to your left.

In the next segment of this exercise, we want you to project yourself mentally inside your living room's south wall, and then conduct four tests. We will test for:

1. Light, intensity, and color
2. Temperature
3. Odor
4. Solidity of material by reflected sound

Remember that we don't wait for things to happen on their own. *You* decide what the distinguishing details will be—you decide what the light is like inside the wall compared to outside the wall. This will be your unique point of reference for the material that your living room's south wall is made of.

Projection into Your Living Room Wall

When you are ready to add the second part of this exercise, then once again enter your level, project yourself mentally to be standing in front of your house, then walk towards your house, go into the house and into your living room, and stand in the center, facing the south wall.

It is nighttime, and the lights are off. Even though the lights are off, you know what is in front of you, (pause) what is behind you. (pause) You know what is to your left, (pause) and to your right. (pause)

Now mentally walk toward the south wall and stand close enough to touch it. (pause) Now objectively—that is, physically—raise your hand to touch the wall.

Objectively stretch out your arm, raise your hand, and, with the palm of your hand, touch the wall. Use your imagination to sense the wall as being smooth or rough, (pause) as cold or warm. (pause) Whatever you perceive with your imagination at this dimension you can use as a point of reference in the future.

Subjectively observe and study the wall from a few inches away. Study the material, (pause) the color. (pause) Whatever you perceive with your imagination at this dimension you can use as a point of reference in the future.

Now I want you to do something you have never done before, something that you cannot do physically, but can only do with your mind:

Imagine projecting yourself subjectively within the wall. (pause) You are now within the wall. You may return your hand to rest on your lap. At this time, we will conduct four tests subjectively. First we will test for light, intensity, and color; our second test is for temperature; the third test is for odor; and the fourth, for solidity of material by reflected sound.

Use your imagination as you do this. There is no right or wrong answer. Whatever you perceive with your imagination in this dimension will be your way of recognizing information from the subjective dimension.

We will now test for light—its intensity and color. Subjectively test for light, intensity, and color; how much light do you sense? (pause) What color do you sense? (pause) Whatever you perceive with your imagination at this dimension you can use as a point of reference in the future.

Now test for temperature. Subjectively test for temperature. (pause) Is there a difference in temperature between the inside and the outside of the wall? (pause) Whatever you perceive with your imagination at this dimension you can use as a point of reference in the future.

Now test for odor. Subjectively test for odor. (pause) Is there a difference in odor between the inside and outside of the wall? (pause) Whatever you perceive with your imagination at this dimension you can use as a point of reference in the future.

Now test for solidity of material by knocking on the inside of the wall. Objectively form a fist and knock on the inside of the subjective wall; objectively raise your hand and go through the motions as you do when you knock on a door. What kind of sound would you expect to hear reflected back to you? How solid would you judge the material to be? Whatever you perceive with your imagination at this dimension you can use as a point of reference in the future.

Now come out of the wall and stand just a few inches away. Now you are at arm's length. Now you are at the center of your living room, facing the south wall.

This concludes the second part of this exercise.

You have practiced entering deep, healthy levels of mind. In your next session, you will enter a deeper, healthier level of mind, faster and easier than this time.

Now when you are ready, count yourself out of your level. Take your time.

Adding to Your Ability in the Subjective Dimension

There are two more segments to this exercise. In the next segment, you will again be standing in the center of your living room facing the south wall, and you will do two things:

First, you will imagine your living room south wall being different colors. It is always good to practice experiencing different colors. In this exercise, what we are doing, in effect, is using colors to expand the bandwidth you can use at this dimension. We will use the primary colors used in electronics. Television sets, computer monitors, and smartphones all use the colors red, green, and blue (abbreviated RGB) to create all other colors. Your brain is an electronic device, so we will use the same RGB colors to expand your subjective capability.

After we have gone through the different colors, then you will examine a chair. You can use any chair you wish. You can mentally lift this chair and move it into any position you desire.

When you are ready, then enter your level and review what you have done thus far. Then continue with the study of colors and with the examination of the chair.

Study Colors and Examine a Chair

When you are ready to add the third part of this exercise, once again enter your level, project yourself mentally to be standing in front of your house, then review what you have done thus far.

You are standing in your living room, facing your south wall. You know the color of your south wall. At this time, change the color of the wall to black. The color of the wall is now black. (pause) You can get a true black color by imagining a painter with a can of black paint and a brush in his hand, painting the wall black and about to finish painting it. (pause)

Your south wall is now all black. Now change it to red. It is now red. (pause) To get a true red color, again imagine the painter about to finish painting it red. (pause) Now change the wall to green. The wall is now green; (pause) imagine it green. Now the wall will be blue. The wall is now blue; imagine it blue. (pause) Now change the wall to violet. The wall is now violet; imagine it violet. (pause) We will change the color back to blue, back to green, back to red, back to black.

We will now mentally examine a chair, selecting any chair we wish. Mentally push it against the black wall. From your position in the center of the living room facing the south wall, mentally lift the chair about 20 degrees above the horizontal plane of sight, in the area of your mental screen.

We will examine the chair, studying its material, (pause) the upholstery, if it is upholstered, and how it is attached to the chair, (pause) and the color of the chair. (pause) Now mentally turn the chair toward the left, (pause) now away from you, (pause) now toward the right, (pause) now facing you. (pause) Whatever you perceive with your imagination at this dimension you can use as a point of reference in the future.

Now change the color of the wall to its actual color. The wall is now its actual color. Again study the chair; how does it stand out against this background? (pause) Whatever you perceive with your imagination at this dimension you can use as a point of reference in the future.

Now change the color of the wall to red. The wall is now red. Study the chair; how does it stand out against a red background? (pause) Whatever you perceive with your imagination at this dimension you can use as a point of reference in the future.

Now change the color of the wall to green. The wall is now green. Study the chair; how does it stand out against a green background? (pause) Whatever you perceive with your imagination at this dimension you can use as a point of reference in the future.

Now change the color of the wall to blue. The wall is now blue. Study the chair; how does it stand out against a blue background? (pause) Whatever you perceive with your imagination at this dimension you can use as a point of reference in the future. The color of the wall will now change back to green, now back to red, now back to the natural color, now back to black. Now cause the chair to disappear from the scene. The chair has disappeared from the scene.

You have practiced entering deep, healthy levels of mind. In your next session, you will enter a deeper, healthier level of mind, faster and easier than this time.

Now when you are ready, count yourself out of your level. Take your time.

Studying Fruits and Vegetables

In the final segment of this exercise, you will examine several fruits and vegetables. These are the fruits and vegetables that were the most popular with José Silva's young research subjects.

When you are ready to add the third part of this exercise, then once again enter your level, project yourself mentally to be standing in front of your house, then review what you have done this far.

You are standing in your living room facing your south wall. The wall is now black; now mentally bring into the scene a watermelon. It will be up against the wall, at the height where we had the chair. Study this watermelon; use your knowing, your memory, your sensing. Above all, use your imagination to study the watermelon. Observe how the green stands out against the black background. (pause)

Now imagine the watermelon cut in half. The watermelon is now cut in half, and you can visualize how the red portion of the watermelon, lined with black seeds, stands out against the white inner rind and the green of the outside. (pause) As you mentally bring the two halves slowly toward you, notice how they appear to increase in size. Examine the various colors: the red, the white, the black, and the green, from only a few inches away. (pause) Now imagine the odor and taste of watermelon. (pause) Whatever you perceive with your imagination at this dimension you can use as a point of reference in the future.

Now cause the watermelon to be near the wall. The watermelon is now near the wall. Now cause the two halves to come together. Now cause the watermelon to disappear from the scene. The watermelon has disappeared from the scene.

Now cause a lemon to appear at the same level, near the wall. A lemon appears in a fluorescent yellow color that stands out against the black wall. (pause) Bring the lemon closer to you, noticing how it appears to increase in size as it approaches. Stop the approaching lemon when it is only a few inches away, and examine its color. (pause) Now imagine the odor and taste of a lemon. (pause) Whatever you perceive with your imagination at this dimension you can use as a point of reference in the future.

Now cause the lemon to be near the wall. The lemon is now near the wall, a little higher than the horizontal level of sight. Now cause the lemon to disappear from the scene. The lemon has disappeared from the scene.

Now cause an orange to appear. An orange has appeared on the scene; observe the color at a distance. (pause) Now bring the orange closer; again observe the color. (pause) Now imagine the odor and taste of an orange. (pause) Whatever you perceive with your imagination at this dimension you can use as a point of reference in the future.

Now cause the orange to be near the wall. The orange is now near the wall. Now cause the orange to disappear from the scene. The orange has disappeared from the scene.

Now cause three bananas to appear. Three bananas have appeared; study the color from far and near. (pause) Now imagine the odor and taste of bananas. (pause) Whatever you perceive with your imagination at this dimension you can use as a point of reference in the future.

Now cause the bananas to be near the wall. Now cause the bananas to disappear from the scene. The bananas have disappeared from the scene.

Now cause three carrots to appear. Three carrots have appeared; study the color from far and near. (pause) Now imagine the odor and taste of carrots. (pause) Whatever you perceive with your imagination at this dimension you can use as a point of reference in the future.

Now cause the carrots to be near the wall. Now cause the carrots to disappear from the scene. The carrots have disappeared from the scene.

Now cause a fresh and crisp head of lettuce to appear. A head of lettuce has appeared; study the color from far. (pause) Now bring it closer and study the color from a distance of about 12 inches. (pause) Whatever you perceive with your imagination at this dimension you can use as a point of reference in the future.

Now cause the head of lettuce to be near the wall. Now cause the head of lettuce to disappear from the scene. The head of lettuce has disappeared from the scene. Whatever you perceive with your imagination at this dimension you can use as points of reference in the future.

It is now an accomplished fact that subjective points of reference have been established at the imaginative dimension, at the subjective dimension, at different levels and different depths. To function at these levels and to use these points of reference, all you need is to have a sincere desire to solve problems.

You have practiced entering deep, healthy levels of mind. In your next session, you will enter a deeper, healthier level of mind, faster and easier than this time.

In your next mental projection exercise, you will establish subjective points of reference in the inanimate matter kingdom: projection into metals.

Now when you are ready, count yourself out of your level. Take your time.

Tips on How to Proceed

Remember to continue to practice the Silva Centering Exercise. We recommend practicing it between each of these mental projection exercises, the same as we do in the live seminars:

X Silva Centering Exercise
X Projection to Home
__ Silva Centering Exercise
__ Projection into Inanimate Matter Kingdom
__ Silva Centering Exercise
__ Projection into Plant Life Kingdom
__ Silva Centering Exercise
__ Projection into Animate Matter Kingdom
__ Silva Centering Exercise
__ Projection into Human Kingdom

After you have completed the training, you can maintain your ability by using what you have learned to solve problems. We recommend that you go to the alpha level at least once a day, for five minutes. Twice a day is better; three times a day is excellent.

To practice for five minutes each time is good, 10 minutes is better, 15 minutes is excellent.

4

Managing Your Energies

You know that business responsibilities and activities can be very stressful, whether you are working for a demanding boss or you have the task of creating income so you can pay the people who work for you.

You also know that too much stress can be very harmful: it can hurt your health; ruin your relationships; curtail your ability to concentrate and learn; lower your productivity, creativity, problem-solving ability; and undermine your self-confidence and happiness.

There are many ways that you can use the alpha level—the inner conscious level—to relieve stress. As we've already seen, just relaxing at alpha for 15 minutes will bring you many benefits. It will strengthen your immune system and protect your health.

During your 15 minutes at alpha, you can think about your tasks for the rest of the day and program to do them well. Alpha is the strongest part of the brain, with the most synchronous and most stable brain frequency, so you can do a better job of analyzing information and making decisions.

You will be safer from accidents, because your mind will automatically use ESP to detect oncoming danger and automatically guide you to the right action to avoid it.

You will be luckier, because your ESP will automatically make you aware of opportunities that 90 percent of people won't know about because they haven't learned to use the subconscious consciously.

You will be more persuasive, because your mind will communicate directly with the people you are trying to persuade.

Relaxing at alpha will help you work more efficiently, so that you will be better able to balance work and family in the midst of demanding job requirements. I am going to have a hard time convincing you of this, but here goes:

Tense situations consume more time per unit of accomplishment than do relaxed situations.

If you react stressfully to a deadline or time limit, your stress interferes with your mental and physical skills. You take more time than you do normally.

If you take as little as five minutes to relax and program yourself positively, those five minutes are saved many times over. What you are doing, in effect, is taking the sting out of the bee— removing the pressure from the time limit.

It all begins with alpha.

The Alpha Room

Now you may be wondering: how can I spend 15 minutes—or even five minutes—at alpha while I am at work? People will think that I am sleeping on the job.

Fortunately, almost every building has a special room where you can go and spend 15 minutes at alpha without anyone disturbing you or wondering what you are doing.

In North America we call it a *rest room*—a bathroom in a public building.

That's right, just go to the bathroom and relax. You can spend a few minutes at alpha before you leave home in the morning, and plan your day. Then another 15-minute session in the rest room after lunch, to correct any mistakes from the morning, and plan the rest of your day. And then 15 minutes before going to sleep at night, to correct any problems you encountered during the day, reinforce your successes, and begin planning for more success tomorrow.

Techniques to Use in Stressful Situations

You have already learned several techniques that you can use when you find yourself in a stressful situation:

- Take a deep breath and as you exhale, relax. A deep breath provides energy, and exhaling is like a "sign of relief" when you relax after a challenging situation.
- Do your 3s. In the Silva Centering Exercise (in chapter 2 and in appendix A), you condition yourself so that the number 3 is associated with physical relaxation, so mentally repeat and visualize the number 3 several times and allow your muscles to relax as you do this.
- Recall your ideal place of relaxation, or any tranquil and passive scenes, to help you relax mentally. You can recall being with your family and enjoying being with them.

- You can also recall previous successes you've had, and recall that feeling of success. This will help you to feel confident and to project that confidence when you speak.

It will take you a few moments to do this, and those few moments often have another benefit: if the stress is due to an interaction you are having with another person, then, when you pause to relax, they probably think that you are analyzing the situation and coming up with a good response. Whatever you say next, they might be more likely to listen to and consider.

The Silva Reprogramming Technique

You can use the subjective dimension to help yourself in many ways. You can improve your energy, your attitude, your health. You can even do the same for others.

Businesspeople experience a variety of complaints that seem to be inherent in the job, a sort of vocational hazard. Frequently, these are vague complaints, not worth mentioning to the family physician, but nevertheless real enough to interfere, to some degree, with the day's work.

Take that early morning feeling. It could be a lethargic feeling. It could be a bad taste in your mouth. It could be a disinclination to face the papers on your desk. It could be the lack of desire to speak to anybody. It could be any number of similar blocks to rolling up your sleeves and pitching in. It might be called the morning blahs.

Shirley L. had them. She was the manager of a women's specialty store, and she felt like crawling into an inventory cabinet each morning. Instead she drank cup after cup of coffee. That helped, but it made her short-tempered with her salespeople the rest of the day.

James S. had them. It took him an hour of sitting at his desk and "waking up" before he could start processing work orders in his printing company.

Here is how they both got rid of the morning blahs once and for all with the Silva techniques.

The first step was to recognize that they were putting up with this morning state and to decide that they were no longer willing to let it interfere with their day.

The second step was to pre-program for a methodology that would work for them.

The third step was to use methodologies like the 5-step method and others that we will describe below.

The Methodology Is a Flexible Tool

Your hands can do anything, when you use them, and with the right tools. Your mind can do anything, when you use it, and with the right tools. Your main tool to combat unwanted attitudes, emotions, personality quirks, listlessness, and boredom is the alpha level.

Other tools at your disposal are visualization and imagination.

In chapter 2, we explained that when you learn to activate your mind and function analytically at the alpha level, you have gained the ability to use the subconscious consciously. In other words, you have created something new, something that José Silva called the *inner conscious level*.

You can use this inner conscious level to correct any problem, at any time. All you need to do is to go to the rest room, or to your car, or any other place where you can go to level for five minutes without being disturbed, and program to correct the problem.

You can use this technique if you feel tired and exhausted and want to be wide awake, feeling fine and in perfect health.

If tension and stress are causing pain in your body—a headache, for instance—you can use this technique.

If you feel insecure or fearful, you can use it to program yourself to feel more confident.

If you get angry and lose your temper and this is interfering with your job performance or your family relationships, you can program yourself at the alpha level to correct this problem.

You can also use deep levels of mind to "rewrite" your personal history. If you feel that you are being limited by events from the past, you can neutralize the effects of this negative past programming at deep levels of mind.

The more you practice entering your level, you will reach deeper levels of mind, and also lower brain frequencies. Soon you will be able to enter the theta brain wave level of 5 cycles per second, where early childhood memories are stored.

When you activate your mind and program to correct problems, your brain will adjust to the alpha level. At theta you can only function inductively; for deductive functioning you need 10 cycles (alpha) or 20 cycles (beta). Alpha is the ideal level for doing your deductive reasoning.

Once you have practiced enough so that you have opened the pathway to theta, the programming that you do at your center—at alpha, the 10-cps center of the normal brain frequency spectrum—will be effective at correcting problems in all parts of the brain.

You can enter your level, identify the problems you want to correct, and correct them using the technique below, as well as the Three Scenes Technique, which you will learn in the next chapter.

A Cautionary Word about Affirmations

We don't use affirmations. In fact, we advise people to be very cautious about using them.

Affirmations are not programming.

According to Webster's dictionary, an affirmation is "an act of saying or showing that something is true."

When people try to "affirm" that they are confident when they aren't, they are not saying something that is true. It's just the opposite: they are lying to themselves. And you know it when you do it.

People who tell you to make those kinds of statements try to justify it by saying that the statements will go into your subconscious. But how can that be true when you are aware—conscious—that you are saying it?

What psychologists named the *subconscious* is the alpha level.

Once you learn to use the alpha level with conscious awareness, it is no longer subconscious for you.

You now know how to use the subconscious consciously.

As José Silva said, that is a contradiction in terms:

If you can use it consciously, then it is no longer *sub*—beneath—consciousness.

That is why we call it the *inner conscious level*.

He coined that term, and he told us that it is the most valuable thing that came from his research: finding a way to use the subconscious consciously.

If you think you have a limiting belief system, or negative past programming that is holding you back, you can use the alpha level to correct it.

There are plenty of courses that will give you techniques to use to work on your problems.

The more attention you pay to your problems, the more you energize the problems. This is why: the harder you try to change, the worse it gets.

We do just the opposite: we solve problems by concentrating on solutions.

Sometimes the past has given you mental blocks, which could hurt you in every way.

So we say, don't think about the past, but only about the present and the future. Don't say it can't be done, but think and act on how to do it.

We move in the direction of our dominant thoughts, so after you have identified the problem, from then on, whenever you think of the problem, recall the solution image you created previously.

Mind guides brain and brain guides body, so when you work on the problem, you are reinforcing the problem. Any time you think of the problem, immediately dismiss that thought—just cancel it out of your consciousness—and replace it with thoughts of the solution.

How Mental Programming Works

A program is a process. If you write and tell me that there is a misspelled word on my website, I can't just affirm that "everything is spelled correctly on my website."

First, I need to know what word is misspelled. Hopefully you will tell me how it is spelled on the site. Then I can find it quickly and correct it.

The Three Scenes Technique, which you will learn in the next chapter, is an excellent way to correct problems. You can use it to change habits and to achieve success in correcting all kinds of problems.

Be sure to keep the Laws of Programming in mind. Selfishness may bring short-term gains, but for long-term prosperity, program to do what is best for everyone concerned.

If you need money to meet your obligations, instead of thinking about the money you are going to make, start off by thinking of what you can do so serve the customer better than other people do.

For guidance, review this statement from the Silva Centering Exercise:

You will continue to take part in constructive and creative activities to make this a better world to live in, so that when we move on, we shall have left behind a better world for those who follow. You will consider the whole of humanity, depending on their ages, as fathers or mothers, brothers or sisters, sons or daughters. You are a superior human being; you have greater understanding, compassion, and patience with others.

Think about that at your level, and you will understand why it is so powerful. If you were repairing an air conditioner for your parents, your siblings, your children, how would you proceed? Do the same for everybody you deal with, and you will soon have all the business you desire.

But a word of caution: don't do it just to make more money. Do it because it is the right thing to do.

As José Silva emphasized:

Do unto others only what you want others to do unto you. If you don't want it done unto you, then don't do it unto others.

Be the kind of person that you would like to do business with. Then other people will want to do business with you.

Better Business on a Spiritual Foundation

We want to do business with people who will help us to solve our problems and succeed in our projects.

We want to do business with people who are honest and truthful with us.

Intuition can help you do all of those things.

You can use your ESP to detect what other people are thinking and how they are feeling. You can learn what their real wants and needs are. You can detect what they are concerned about and what they fear.

When you do this, you can offer them more value, because you can create a solution that is exactly what they want and need.

In addition to using your natural, God-given intuition to detect information about other people—information that you can use to help you develop a perfect solution for their problems—you can also put ideas into their mind.

You can let them know that you are honest and sincere and that they can trust you and depend on you.

But a word of caution: you'd better be telling the truth, because they will know if you aren't. If there is something inside of you that wants to take advantage of them, they will sense it.

When you go to them with a proposal that is exactly what they have been hoping for, and they feel that you are honest and will do what you promise, and that you understand them and their situation better than the other people who are submitting proposals to them, then they will do business with you.

If you have an old belief system that you don't deserve to succeed, or that you are not smart enough or good enough, then prove to yourself that you *do* deserve to succeed and that you are good enough by making the best proposals and providing more value than anybody else.

The alpha brain-wave level is the ideal level to do your thinking. Once you learn how remain at the alpha level to do your thinking, then you can analyze the entire situation. If you detect that you are doing something that hinders the process and might keep the client from enjoying the benefits and value that you can provide, then you can easily change whatever that is.

If you have some kind of mental block, there is a reason you have it. Even if you identify it, whatever caused you to develop it in the first place might make it very difficult for you to fix.

If you sincerely want to provide great value to the other party, and be fairly compensated for your efforts, then your mind will find a way to help make it happen. There is no need to go digging up old problems.

Just concentrate on solutions.

José Silva's research indicates that we were sent to planet earth to solve problems and improve living conditions.

José Silva said to provide something of value—goods or services—and "keep in mind what your needs are, plus a little bit more."

He used to tell us that if you need a million dollars, it is easy to get it: just give ten million dollars in service to humanity.

When you are taking part in constructive and creative activities to make this a better world to live in—and keep in mind what your needs are—then you will succeed.

José Silva's UltraMind ESP System is the only scientifically researched and proven system that we know of that helps you learn to use your natural, God-given intuition to do exactly that.

Learning to use your intuition (also known as ESP, psychic ability, clairvoyance, etc.) is a new skill. As with any other new skill, you need to practice it a few minutes every day to develop your expertise.

Five Steps to Success

There are five steps to correcting problems. These are applied at the alpha level, so first enter the alpha level, then use these five steps:

1. In order to correct a problem, you must first identify the problem. You can tell yourself mentally: "I am tired and exhausted"; "I feel tired and exhausted"; or "I have a headache."

2. Mentally state the solution: "I want to be wide awake, feeling fine and in perfect health," or "I want to be pain-free."

3. Make a plan: "In a moment I am going to count from 1 to 5, and at the count of 5 I will open my eyes, be wide awake, feeling fine and in perfect health." If you are doing this to relieve a headache or other pain, say mentally, "I will have no headache, I will feel no headache, and this is so."

4. Work your plan. Count slowly from 1 to 5. At the count of 3, remind yourself of the solution: "At the count of 5, I will open my eyes and be wide awake, feeling fine and in perfect health." Add that you will feel energized, will feel no pain, will feel confident, or will have no anger, etc.

5. When you reach the count of 5 and open your eyes, assume that you have succeeded, that the technique has worked. Even if you don't feel that it has worked yet, act *as if* it has already worked. This is what is called an "assumptive close" in sales: assume success; act as if it were already a done deal. If you check to see if you are still tired, or if you still have the headache, you'll find it. So act as if it were gone, and it will be gone.

Sometimes serious problems require more than one application. For severe pain, such as a migraine headache, use three applications, five minutes apart. Each application will correct more of the problem until the problem is completely gone.

Always remember to take it for granted that the correction has taken place. Act *as if* you have already achieved what you programmed for, even if does not seem to have taken place yet. When you do this, your mind will know that you are serious, and will respond appropriately.

Other People Resonate with You

If you feel tired and listless and have no energy, you are affecting others that you work with. It makes no difference if you are hiding in your office. The energy that your body radiates penetrates walls and crosses distances.

If you are enthusiastic and vibrant, you are also affecting others you work with. Yes, they are affected by hearing you and seeing you, but even without the benefit of these senses, their own spirits are lifted by yours.

So it is important to you as a businessperson to be able to use the alpha level to correct your own deficiencies in attitude, energy, or health, not for just personal reasons but for the benefit of everyone you come into contact with.

The more that others respect your position and the more rapport you have with them, the more they respond positively to you.

You have more of a responsibility to keep yourself in top physical and mental shape than does a less influential person. The alpha level is your control. At 10 cycles per second, your brain waves are at a normalizing harmony.

Mental Rehearsal

You know the saying: practice makes perfect. Practicing mentally at the alpha brain-wave level is almost as beneficial as practicing physically.

To take advantage of this, enter the alpha level and project yourself mentally to the place where you will be carrying out the action. Study your surroundings, become familiar with them. Preparation leads to success—often the one who is best prepared is the one who wins.

If you want to improve your golf game, you need to practice swinging golf clubs and hitting balls. It doesn't matter where you are. The great golfer Lee Trevino said if the weather is bad and you can't go outside, then get up out of your comfortable reclining chair, pick up a wedge, and practice chipping wiffle balls into the recliner.

Practicing a presentation mentally will strengthen your mental memory in the same way that hitting golf balls will reinforce your muscular memory.

If you want to be mentally strong—to develop your mental powers—then practice mentally at the alpha level.

You can use this technique to help you perform better, make a better presentation, be more persuasive, be a better speaker, a better listener, or whatever you need that will help you to serve your customers better.

Practicing at Level

Once you have entered your level and projected yourself mentally to the place where you will do your job, imagine yourself performing the way you desire.

Notice how you feel each step of the way, and imagine your ability improving all the time.

Imagine your mental faculties becoming so keen that you can automatically anticipate any situation, any question, any task that needs to be performed.

You can rehearse the complete event with your imagination in this manner. At the end, imagine yourself being congratulated for your performance.

Mental rehearsal is excellent to use either before or after an activity or event.

After the event, you can enter your level and correct any problems you had so that you will perform better next time. Identify the problem, then do it again with your imagination, but this time do it better than before. Let your final thoughts be of success and accomplishments.

Whenever you have a success, enter your level as soon as possible. Review your performance and recall how you felt when you were successful.

Then, when you are ready to mentally rehearse a new activity, go to your center. Recall your success, and the special feeling that you had when you had this success. This will help you to be just as successful again, and even more successful in the future.

The Formula for Mental Rehearsal

Here is the complete formula:

When you have an activity to perform and you desire to rehearse it mentally ahead of time, go to your center with the 3 to 1 Method (the standard way of entering the alpha level that you learned in chapter 2), and project yourself mentally to the location where you will perform the activity.

Once you have projected yourself mentally to the place where you will perform the activity, imagine yourself performing the way you desire. Imagine yourself improving and accomplishing your task successfully.

Notice how you feel as you are performing the task. Imagine how you feel as you begin the activity the way that you desire. Imagine how you feel as you progress in the activity. Imagine feeling successful, and imagine a sense of accomplishment as you succeed at your assigned task.

When you are done, count yourself out of level.

Projection into the Kingdom of Inanimate Matter

Now we will continue with your ESP training by learning Effective Sensory Projection into the kingdom of inanimate matter. You will study metals from a subjective point of view.

Start by getting four different metal objects. We recommend stainless steel, copper, brass, and aluminum. Then we want you to handle the metals and become familiar with them physically, because this makes it easier for you to project yourself into them mentally, the way you projected yourself into your living room's south wall in the previous chapter.

First, you use your physical senses to study each object. What does it look like? What does it feel like? Can you detect an odor?

After you study each metal, bring it to your forehead, and touch your forehead with it. When you do, close your eyes and make an impression. This is the procedure we will use when you project yourself mentally into each of the metals.

After you enter your level, you will review those objective impressions at the subjective alpha level. This will make it easier for you to then project your subjective senses—your mind—to detect subjective information and relate it to the objective impressions you made with your physical senses.

Conduct the four tests. Remember that you are projecting, which means that *you* make it happen.

José Silva said that, "Whatever you imagine, that is what counts here."

That is the key: We don't wait to "perceive" something; we take action and use imagination to imagine what we would experience.

Why inanimate matter first? Because that is the simplest structure—just atoms and molecules. Whenever you learn something new, you start with the basics, and then add complexity. For instance, in business, you need to know basic math—how to add, subtract, multiply, divide. Then you know that when a customer orders three widgets for $2 each, you multiply: 3 x 2 = $6.

When you learn that the $6 is considered income, and the $1 each that the widgets cost you is considered expense, then you will be able to understand a profit-and-loss statement.

Once you learn about assets and liabilities and equity, you can learn to read a balance sheet and other financial documents that are important to a business. But if somebody tries to explain a balance sheet to you before you understand the basics, it won't make any sense to you.

So we are going to start with the simplest structures in physics: inanimate objects. Inanimate objects are composed of atoms and molecules. The ancient Greeks said that the atom was the basic building block of matter. You can combine atoms in a certain way to make something more complex: molecules.

After we project mentally into the inanimate kingdom and gain some experiences detecting metals, then we will move up to the plant life kingdom. This is a giant leap forward: it combines atoms and molecules into something entirely different: cells. That's life! Cells can reproduce.

The next step: Combine cells together in a certain way and you have organs: a heart, a brain, a kidney. We will study the anatomy of a pet.

The final step is the highest life form on the planet: the human being, so we will study human anatomy from a psychic point of view.

A human being is made up of organ systems. These are made up of organs, which in turn are made up of cells, which are made up of molecules, which are made up of atoms, which are made up of subatomic particles, which are derived from pure spiritual energy.

These are what we call the *building blocks of matter.*

Later, when you begin practicing and developing proficiency with your psychic ability, it will be easiest to start by detecting serious problems in human beings. While the human body is quite complex, a human being has more intelligence than an animal or a plant or an inanimate object, and that makes it easier to detect problems.

Projecting to the inanimate matter kingdom requires the most from us. We must project all the way, because inanimate matter does not have any intelligence to come part of the way towards us.

Plant life has some intelligence, and can meet us partway.

Animal life has still more intelligence and can come further towards us. The human kingdom has the most intelligence and can meet us halfway. That is why it is easiest to practice first detecting serious human health problems.

During the conditioning cycle, you will enter the alpha brain-wave level and review your objective impressions. Then you will use mental projection to establish subjective points of reference by projecting your mind inside the metals.

Remember to use your hands; this will produce a more vivid experience for you.

Remember that we do not wait passively to perceive something. We *project* in order to achieve the most effective experience.

Practical Applications

Our main purpose right now is to familiarize yourself with all aspects of the subjective dimension so that you will be a better psychic. But there are some practical applications for this intimate knowledge of the kingdom of inanimate matter.

Suppose that your job involves maintenance of equipment or machinery. When something breaks down, you can project your mind into it and mentally determine the location of the problem.

If you need to determine whether the problem is with a steel shaft, for instance, or with a copper bushing around that shaft, you can use your points of reference to find out. At your level, project your mind to the problem area and recall your previous experiences:

Is the amount and quality of the light more like steel or more like copper? Use the Alternate Choice technique: recall your previous experience of light within steel, then within copper. Go back and forth a few times and determine which is most likely.

Then in order to confirm what you find, do the same with your previous experiences with temperature, odor, and solidity of material: recall one, then the other, back and forth, until you feel confident that you know which one it is.

Sam Gonzalez Silva, who now lives in Las Vegas, Nevada, is José Silva's nephew. When Sam was growing up, he lived next door to José, and he learned at an early age how to use his ESP—his intuition—just as naturally as his other senses. It proved very useful to him later when he was in the Air Force.

Sam's job was to maintain and repair complex electronic equipment. One afternoon when he went into work, the man he relieved was tired and frustrated because he had spent the entire shift trying to troubleshoot and debug a piece of equipment.

Sam took over the task, relaxed, and projected his mind into the piece of equipment in order to mentally detect anything that wasn't the way it should be.

It was as if he were daydreaming. He could imagine any part of the equipment. He didn't need to see it with his eyes, because he could visualize it with his mind.

It only took Sam a few minutes to locate a circuit that didn't match what he expected to find. There was something abnormal about it.

So he focused his eyes on the equipment, opened it up, went to the problem area, and fixed it.

In just a few minutes he was able to find and correct a problem that a person who didn't know how to use his ESP had failed to do in an entire eight-hour shift.

Imagine how valuable a skill like that can be to your business. Imagine how valuable it can be when you are developing something new and need to get all the bugs out and make it work as efficiently as possible.

After Sam got out of the Air Force, he began teaching the Silva Mind Control course.

Establishing Points of Reference with People You Meet

José Silva's brother Juan used to advise that we establish objective points of reference about new people when we meet them.

Notice what they look like, what their voice sounds like, how their hand feels when you shake hands with them. Later when you want to program to help that person or to work on your relationship with them, you can enter your level and recall the previous impressions that you made—the points of reference. This will help you to recall more about them.

If they give you something, like a business card or a brochure for instance, you can also use this to help you attune to them later. We will explain exactly how to do that in chapter 7, when we cover psychometry.

Where to Find Metals to Practice With

You can easily find objects around the house that you can use, and also at your local hardware store.

You probably have many stainless-steel items around the house. Most people use stainless flatware: knives and forks and spoons, as well as pots and pans, scissors, and tools.

Copper is easy too. Maybe you have an old copper pot or tea kettle, or a candlestick, wire, or plumbing fixtures made of copper.

Musical instruments, bells, and some medallions, keys, and belt buckles are made of brass, as are certain decorative items and plaques.

Aluminum is very common and easy to find: kitchen items, thermos bottles, aluminum cans, and window frames.

Your local hardware store will have everything you need: copper pipe and copper tubing, as well as copper and brass fittings and couplings that are used in plumbing work. They also have both stainless-steel and brass screws and bolts. You can often buy these for less than $1.

You could also visit a gift shop and see if there are any brass or copper items you'd like to have for your house. If you want a brass bell at your front door, that will also provide you with a metal to use.

You can use other metals too, instead of or in addition to these. Many people like to use precious metals—gold and silver, for instance. The more points of reference you establish, the better.

Handle each object, turn it around and look at it from all sides, smell it, bring it to your forehead and let it touch your forehead, close your eyes, and make an impression.

Then, during the condition cycle, you will repeat those movements before projecting yourself mentally into the metal.

Projection into Metals

Remember to handle each metal while at beta. Notice what it looks like, what it feels like, how heavy it is, how solid it feels, any odor it might have. You do not need to hold the metal during the conditioning cycle, but please do use your hands as if you were handling it. When you use your hands and imagine touching the object physically, it will help you detect information about it mentally, in the subjective (nonphysical) dimension.

When you are ready, enter your level as you learned to do in chapter 2. Then project yourself mentally to the living room in your home and imagine yourself standing in the center, facing the south wall.

Then extend your arm objectively and visualize the piece of stainless steel. Mentally sense the piece of stainless steel, and relive and objectively repeat all the movements made previously. (pause) Bring the steel closer and closer to your forehead; mentally observe it a few inches away. (pause)

Now allow the stainless steel to touch your forehead, and mentally project yourself into it. (pause) You are now within the piece of stainless steel. You may return your hand to rest on your lap. (pause) If you imagine the piece of stainless steel to be just big enough for you to fit in, you will not go very deeply inside, but if you imagine the piece of steel to be as big as a room, then you can go further within. If you imagine this piece of steel to be as large as a massive building, and feel your size in contrast with it, then you can go still further within, using the depth offered by this dimension of mind.

Whenever you need to increase the illumination or amount or size of anything, just snap the fingers of your *right* hand slightly and expect the change to take place. For a decrease, or to return anything back to its original state, snap the fingers of your *left* hand slightly, and expect the change to take place. Whatever you perceive with your imagination at this dimension you can use as points of reference in the future.

At this time we are going to subjectively conduct four tests. The first test will be for light, intensity, and color. Sense the intensity and color of light within the stainless steel. (pause) Whatever you perceive with your imagination at this dimension you can use as a point of reference in the future.

At the count of 3, we will test for temperature. Sense the temperature within the stainless steel. (pause) Whatever you perceive with your imagination at this dimension you can use as a point of reference in the future.

At the count of 3, we will test for odor. Sense the odor within the stainless steel. (pause) Whatever you perceive with your imagination at this dimension you can use as a point of reference in the future.

At the count of 3, we will test for solidity of material by knocking on the stainless steel. Physically form a fist and go through the motions of knocking on the stainless steel, as you do on a wall. (pause) What kind of sound do you subjectively hear? (pause) Whatever you perceive with your imagination at this dimension you can use as a point of reference in the future.

Now objectively touch your forehead and come out of the stainless steel. Objectively extend your arm and allow the imaginary piece of steel to float in space by itself, at a level a little higher than the horizontal plane, or level, of sight. You may return your hand to rest on your lap.

How does the piece of stainless steel stand out against the natural color of the wall? Keep the piece of stainless steel rotating in your imagination; keep it moving; keep it dynamic. (pause)

Now the color of the wall will change to red. The wall is now red. Keep the piece of steel rotating, noticing how it stands out against the red background. (pause)

Now the color of the wall will change to green. The wall is now green. Notice how the piece of rotating steel stands out against the green background. (pause)

Now the color of the wall will change to blue. The wall is now blue. Notice how the piece of rotating steel stands out against the blue background. (pause)

The color of the wall will now change back to green, back to red, back to the actual color of the wall. Now the piece of stainless steel will disappear from the scene. The piece of stainless steel has disappeared from the scene.

Now we will play back the impressions made with copper. Extend your arm objectively and mentally play back the previous impressions made with copper. Repeat every movement; bring your hand closer and closer. (pause)

Now touch your forehead, and mentally project yourself into the piece of copper. (pause) In your imagination you are now within the piece of copper, at any depth you desire. You may return your hand to rest on your lap. Remember to use your finger-snapping controls to increase and decrease size as necessary.

Now we will conduct the first test. Sense the intensity and color of light within copper. (pause) How does the light within copper compare with that of stainless steel? (pause) Whatever you perceive with your imagination at this dimension you can use as a point of reference in the future.

Now test for temperature. Sense the temperature within copper. (pause) How does the temperature of copper compare with that of stainless steel? (pause) Whatever you perceive with your imagination at this dimension you can use as a point of reference in the future.

Now test for odor. Sense the odor within copper. (pause) How does the odor of copper compare with that of stainless steel? (pause) Whatever you perceive with your imagination at this dimension you can use as a point of reference in the future.

Now test for solidity of material. Objectively form a fist and knock on copper. (pause) How does the imagined sound of copper compare with that of stainless steel? (pause) Whatever you perceive with your imagination at this dimension, you can use as a point of reference in the future.

Now touch your forehead to come out of the piece of copper; you are now coming out of the copper. Extend your arm and hold the piece of copper at arm's length. Now allow the piece of copper to float in space, using as a background the natural color of your living room's south wall. Keep the piece of copper rotating. You may return your hand to rest on your lap. (pause)

Now the color of the wall will change to red. The wall is now red. How does this piece of copper stand out against a red background? (pause) How does this compare with the piece of stainless steel? Keep the piece of copper rotating. (pause)

Now the color of the wall will change to green. The wall is now green. How does this piece of copper stand out against a green background? (pause) How does this compare with the stainless steel? Keep the piece of copper rotating. (pause)

Now the color of the wall will change to blue. The wall is now blue. How does this piece of copper stand out against a blue background? (pause) How does this compare with the stainless steel? Keep the piece of copper rotating. (pause)

The color of the wall will now change back to green, back to red, back to the actual color of the wall. Now the piece of copper will disappear from the scene. The piece of copper has disappeared from the scene.

Now we will visualize the piece of brass. Extend your arm objectively and visualize the piece of brass, reliving all your previous movements as you bring your hand closer and closer. (pause)

Now touch your forehead, and mentally project yourself into the brass. (pause) You are now within the brass at any depth or level you desire. You may return your hand to rest on your lap.

At the count of 3, we will conduct the first test. Sense the intensity and color of light within brass. (pause) How does the light within brass compare with that of copper (pause) and stainless steel? (pause) Whatever you perceive with your imagination at this dimension you can use as a point of reference in the future.

Now test for temperature. Sense the temperature within brass. (pause) How does the temperature of brass compare with that of copper (pause) and stainless steel? (pause) Whatever you perceive with your imagination at this dimension you can use as a point of reference in the future.

Now test for odor. Sense the odor within brass. (pause) How does the odor of brass compare with that of copper (pause) and stainless steel? (pause) Whatever you perceive with your imagination at this dimension you can use as a point of reference in the future.

Now test for solidity of material. Objectively form a fist and knock on brass. (pause) How does the reflected sound of brass compare with that of copper (pause) and stainless steel? (pause) Whatever you perceive with your imagination at this dimension you can use as a point of reference in the future.

Now touch your forehead to come out of the piece of brass. Touch your forehead; you are now coming out of the brass. Extend your arm and hold the piece of brass at arm's length. Now allow the piece of brass to float in space, using as a background the natural color of your living room's south wall. Keep the piece of brass rotating. You may return your hand to rest on your lap. (pause)

Now the color of the wall will change to red. The wall is now red. How does this piece of brass stand out against a red background? (pause) How does this compare with the piece of copper (pause) and the piece of stainless steel? Keep the piece of brass rotating. (pause)

Now the color of the wall will change to green. The wall is now green. How does this piece of brass stand out against a green background? (pause) How does this compare with the copper (pause) and stainless steel? Keep the piece of brass rotating. (pause)

Now the color of the wall will change to blue. The wall is now blue. How does this piece of brass stand out against a blue background? (pause) How does this compare with the copper (pause) and stainless steel? Keep the piece of brass rotating. (pause)

The color of the wall will now change back to green, back to red, back to the actual color of the wall. Now the piece of brass will disappear from the scene. (snap fingers) The piece of brass has disappeared from the scene.

Now we will visualize the piece of aluminum. Extend your arm objectively and visualize the piece of aluminum, reliving all your previous movements, bringing your hand closer and closer. (pause) Now touch your forehead and mentally project yourself into the piece of aluminum. (pause) You are now within the piece of aluminum, at any depth or level you desire. You may return your hand to rest on your lap.

Now we will conduct the first test. Sense the intensity and color of light within aluminum. (pause) How does the light within aluminum compare with that of brass, (pause) copper, (pause) and stainless steel? (pause) Whatever you perceive with your imagination at this dimension you can use as a point of reference in the future.

Now test for temperature. Sense the temperature within aluminum. (pause) How does the temperature of aluminum compare with that of brass, (pause) copper, (pause) and stainless steel? (pause) Whatever you perceive with your imagination at this dimension you can use as a point of reference in the future.

Now test for odor. Sense the odor within aluminum. (pause) How does the odor of aluminum compare with that of brass, (pause) copper, (pause) and stainless steel? (pause) Whatever you perceive with your imagination at this dimension you can use as a point of reference in the future.

Now test for solidity of material. Objectively form a fist and knock on the aluminum. (pause) How does the reflected sound of aluminum compare with that of brass, (pause) copper, (pause) and stainless steel? (pause) Whatever you perceive with your imagination at this dimension you can use as a point of reference in the future.

Now touch your forehead to come out of the piece of aluminum. Touch your forehead; you are now coming out of the aluminum. Extend your arm and hold the piece of aluminum at arm's length. Now allow the piece of aluminum to float in space, using as a background the natural color of your living room's south wall. Keep the piece of aluminum rotating. You may return your hand to rest on your lap. (pause)

Now the color of the wall will change to red. The wall is now red. How does the piece of aluminum stand out against a red background? (pause) How does this compare with the brass, (pause) copper, (pause) and stainless steel? Keep the piece of aluminum rotating. (pause)

Now the color of the wall will change to green. The wall is now green. How does this piece of aluminum stand out against a green background? (pause) How does this compare with brass, (pause) copper, (pause) and stainless steel? Keep the piece of aluminum rotating. (pause)

Now the color of the wall will change to blue. The wall is now blue. How does this piece of aluminum stand out against a blue background? (pause) How does this compare with the brass, (pause) copper, (pause) and stainless steel? Keep the piece of aluminum rotating. (pause)

The color of the wall will now change back to green, back to red, back to the actual color of the wall. Now the piece of aluminum will disappear from the scene (snap fingers). The piece of aluminum has disappeared from the scene. Whatever you perceive with your imagination at this dimension you can use as points of reference in the future.

It is now an accomplished fact that subjective points of reference have been established in the kingdom of inanimate matter at different levels and different depths. To function at these levels and to use these points of reference, all you need is to have a sincere desire to solve problems. Your mind will automatically seek out these points of reference, where you will perceive and become aware of information you can use to solve such problems. And this is so.

You have practiced entering deep, healthy levels of mind. In your next session, you will enter a deeper, healthier level of mind, faster and easier than this time.

In the next exercise, you will establish points of reference in the plant life kingdom by projection to a tree and a study of leaves.

Now when you are ready, count yourself out of your level. Take your time.

Tips on How to Proceed

Remember to continue to practice the Silva Centering Exercise. We recommend practicing it between each of these mental projection exercises, just as we do in our live seminars:

 X Silva Centering Exercise

 X Projection to Home

 X Silva Centering Exercise

 X Projection into Inanimate Matter Kingdom

 — Silva Centering Exercise

 — Projection into Plant Life Kingdom

 — Silva Centering Exercise

 — Projection into Animate Matter Kingdom

 — Silva Centering Exercise

 — Projection into Human Kingdom

After you have completed the training, then you can maintain your ability by using what you have learned to solve problems. We recommend that you go to the alpha level at least once a day, for five minutes. Twice a day is better; three times a day is excellent.

To practice for five minutes each time is good, 10 minutes is better, 15 minutes is excellent.

5

Correcting Problems with Visualization and Imagination

People with the clearest vision of their objectives are the most likely to achieve those objectives.

We are guided by our inner images. But only 20 percent of people are natural visualizers. The other 80 percent *think* about what they want, they *talk* to themselves about what they want, but they don't *create mental pictures* to guide themselves and others as they strive to achieve success.

Henry Ford envisioned a car in every garage, and Bill Gates envisioned a computer in every home. Steve Jobs' visions included great detail, and he wasn't satisfied until the reality matched the pictures he had in his mind.

The good news is that you can improve your ability to create detailed mental pictures and project your visions to other people. You already started when you went through the Projection to Home exercise in chapter 3: You stood outside your home mentally and studied details of how it looks. You studied colors. Then you went inside and studied details in your living room.

You continued studying details in chapter 4, when you studied metals, and you created new visions when you imagined the metals against different color backgrounds. Going through the color spectrum the way you did—from red to green to blue—expanded the "bandwidth" that is available to you mentally.

José Silva had a very simple recommendation for improving your ability to create vivid, detailed mental pictures: take a memory course. In his old Silva Mind Control course, he even included part of a memory course that he learned from Dr. Bruno Furst's Course in Memory and Concentration. There are other books by Harry Lorayne and others that you can choose from. The key is to picture what you want to remember, and associate it with something you are already familiar with.

You can remember names by creating a mental image associated with the name, and associating the image with the person in some way. Often you can just ask a person how to remember their name. Ed Bernd Jr. will tell you: "I am Son Burned. My dad is Dad Burned. My mother is just Burned Up." Combine that with his reddish complexion, and it is easy to remember.

If you want someone to do something, project a mental picture to them of them doing it while you talk to them, and they are more likely to do it. You can use this when persuading a customer to buy your products or services, when managing employees, when negotiating a deal that both parties will gain from, and even when talking with your teenage children.

To learn more, get any memory course that uses mental imagery and practice it. If you do not normally project mental images to people when you are interacting with them, then you can enter the alpha level and program yourself to do so. This one simple thing can make you more persuasive, and can open up a whole new world of success for you.

José Silva's Formula for Acquiring Wealth

People often ask us how to acquire money. Some people claim they can teach you how to "manifest" money. I don't even know what that means. Money is not a thing; it is a medium of exchange, a means of keeping score.

If you don't have enough money to pay your bills and take care of your family, that is a problem. Getting enough money to pay your bills and take care of your family is a problem. It is not a solution.

There is a very important principle to remember: *our inner images create our outer reality. We move in the direction of our dominant thoughts.* In other words, mind guides brain, and brain guides body.

That means you don't solve problems by concentrating on the problems. We solve problems by concentrating on solutions.

If the problem is getting money to pay your bills and care for your family, then the solution is the bills being paid and your family having what they need.

Would you like to know what José Silva did when he needed money?

"I would enter my level," he told us, "and start thinking about what new product I could create, or what new service I could provide, that people would benefit from and would be willing to pay for.

"Then," he added," I would keep in mind what my needs are, plus a little bit more.

"The bigger your plans are—meaning how many people will benefit—the bigger your needs are. Big plans mean you have big needs."

When you do that, you will qualify for help from higher intelligence. We will give you the formula for that in the next chapter.

Notice that the people we mentioned a few minutes ago— Henry Ford, Bill Gates, Steve Jobs—did envision themselves having millions of dollars. But they also envisioned millions of people benefitting from the products they created and the services they provided. They didn't ignore the fact that they needed money in order to turn their visions into reality. It is important to keep in mind what your needs are, plus a little bit more.

When they envisioned doing things that would improve people's lives—putting a car in every garage, a computer in every home, a smartphone in every pocket—they caught the attention of higher intelligence and got the help they needed to change the world for the better. In the next chapter we'll explain how you can do the same thing.

Always concentrate on solutions. Whenever you think of the problem—the unpaid bills, for instance—let that thought go, erase that image. Think about the solution; recall your vision for helping humanity by improving living conditions on the planet.

José Silva had a very simple formula for getting a million dollars: "If you need a million dollars," he said, "it is easy to get it: Just give 10 million dollars' worth of service to humanity, and if you need a million dollars, you will get it."

He emphasized the word *need*. Higher intelligence isn't going to help us if we just want to indulge ourselves. He explained that in instructor training one year, when one of the new Silva instructors asked if it was OK to program to get a Rolls-Royce automobile:

"You are asking a good question," Mr. Silva replied. "He's asking for a Rolls-Royce. This is in the possibility area.

"But you see, we were not sent on a vacation. We're not going to get help from the other side when we want something like this only for me.

"But if I say that I want this vehicle, so that *we* can use it—*we*, not just me—because there is a need for something like this, and it's within the possibility area, and I don't have the means, then I may persuade the other side to help me.

"Now the other side will only help me when I am asking for something that is needed to improve conditions on planet earth.

"They are not going to help me if I want another million dollars when I already have a million dollars, when I want a Rolls-Royce when I have a Rolls-Royce already. If I want a girlfriend when I already have a wife. Some people ask for something like this.

"They are not going to help you. You are on your own. If you make a mistake, you are going to suffer for it; you are on your own. You don't get help from the other side.

"You only get help from the other side when your intentions are that whatever you are doing is to help improve conditions on the planet for more than yourself, not just yourself.

"If you only consider *me, me,* you have to do it on your own. If it is for *us,* then you get help, if whatever you do is going to help more than you. The more you are going to help, the more help you get for it.

"We always say, don't ever ask for more than what you need, but *do* ask for *no less* than what you need.

"So what your needs will be depends on how big your plans are. That's what your needs will be," he concluded.

How Mona Salem Doubled Her Sales

Mona Salem had been selling real estate in California for more than 20 years with just average results. Then she learned the Silva UltraMind ESP System and did some alpha thinking that doubled her results and quadrupled her confidence. Here is what she told us:

I have been a real estate agent for 23+ years. In the past, I had one listing, sell it and close escrow, and hunt around for another listing. So at this rate, I maxed out at five listings a year.

I recently got a listing. I was really excited about it, since it was the first listing in eight months. I used this excitement as point of reference and thought about it a lot at level. Lo and behold, I got another listing appointment. The seller said that he would get back to me. He emailed me a day or two later and asked me for references. I gave him three. I felt that this would not clinch the listing, so I went to level to think about things.

I came up with a great idea. A photographer had recently come to my broker's office and made a presentation on a 3D house tour using photos. It was fabulous, and I was impressed. It cost $500.

I proceeded to act on my intuition and sent links of a number of house tours (the photographer gave me these links) to my potential seller. He said, "Wow. We want you to be our realtor."

Now I have two listings (they are both in escrow). I have never, ever in my 23+ year career had two listings at the same time. This is proof positive that feeling excited and great about my first listing precipitated another.

I am working on getting a third listing in the same way. My intuition seems to be telling me to expand my area or "farm," as we say in real estate.

Visualization and Imagination Defined

Silva techniques will bring about changes for the better in every area of your life: health, relationships, business, learning, self-confidence—anything you desire to change.

Why do they work so well? What mechanisms are involved in making these changes?

The key is functioning in the subjective (mental) dimension. When you enter your level, you are functioning in the invisible world of the mind, and you are able to make changes in the visible world of the body.

The tools of the subjective dimension are visualization and imagination. They are two faculties of genius. Let's take a close look at these tools so you will understand exactly what they are and how to use them in the subjective dimension to make the needed changes.

Remember that it is important to use visualization and imagination in the subjective dimension, that is, at your level. Many books tell you to visualize your goals, but if they do not teach you a method for doing so in the subjective dimension, then this will do you little good.

You only see with your physical eyes, your eyesight. When your eyes are closed, you can't see anything, because you are not using your eyes. If you are trying to see something when you visualize, you will go to the beta brain frequency. You do not want to do this. You need to be at the alpha frequency in order to use ESP and to program.

So you *see* with your *eyes*, you *visualize* with your *mind*. That is, you recall to mind what something looks like.

Visualization is memory. Visualization is remembering what something looks like. Visualization is a receiving mechanism. In the subjective dimension, you receive a mental image of what something looks like. If your mental image is not as clear as you would like, simply recall what the subject looks like. Recalling what something looks like is visualization. Recall the details and the colors, just as you did when in chapter 3 you studied the front of your home and then studied your living-room wall and items in your living room.

Imagination is a creative process. With imagination, you create a mental image of something you have not seen previously. With imagination, you create whatever you desire, the way you did when you imagined a painter painting your living room wall black, and then imagined it being painted other colors.

When you create something in the subjective dimension, with your imagination, then it actually exists—in the subjective dimension—and can be perceived by other people when they are functioning in the subjective dimension.

Everything must first be created in the subjective dimension; then it can manifest in the physical (objective) dimension also.

Imagination is a transmitting mechanism. With imagination, you can transmit your desired end result to the physical dimension.

There is no time or space in the subjective dimension. When you create something, it exists as of that moment. But the physical dimension does have time and space, so it may take time before your desires manifest physically.

Visualization is the receiving mechanism; imagination is the transmitting mechanism. How do you put these to use?

You can use the Three Scenes Technique. But first it's time to become aware of your Mental Screen.

The Mental Screen

Even with eyes closed, if you attempt to use them to see something, your brain will go to 20 cycles beta. That is why Mr. Silva created the Mental Screen. He found that some people were trying to "see" an image on the back of their eyelids, and that brought them out of alpha, even though their eyes were still closed.

Alpha is the ideal place to do your mental work, so it is important that you not try to focus your eyes and "see" anything when you need to function at alpha. Here is how to use your Mental Screen.

To locate your Mental Screen, begin with your eyes closed, turned slightly upward from the horizontal plane of sight, at an angle of approximately 20 degrees.

The area that you perceive with your mind is your Mental Screen.

Without using your eyelids as screens, sense your Mental Screen to be out, away from your body.

To improve the use of your Mental Screen, project images or mental pictures onto the screen, especially images having color. Concentrate on mentally sensing and visualizing true color.

The Three Scenes Technique

When you desire to use the Three Scenes Technique, go to your center with the 3 to 1 Method. Using visualization, create and project onto your Mental Screen, directly in front of you, an image of the existing situation.

Recall details of what the situation looks like in this first scene. Make a good study of the existing situation so that you are completely aware of all aspects of it.

If you have programmed for this project previously, then take into account any changes that have taken place since your most recent programming session.

After making a good study of the existing situation, then shift your awareness to your left approximately 15 degrees. In a second scene, to the left of the first scene, use imagination to mentally picture yourself taking action and doing something to implement your decisions and to follow the guidance you have received, and imagine the desired changes beginning to take place.

Now in the third scene, another 15 degrees farther to your left, use your imagination to create and project an image of the situation the way you desire for it to end up. Imagine many people benefitting. The more people who benefit, the better.

Anytime in the future when you think of this project, visualize—recall—the image that you created of the desired end result in the third scene.

You can use the Three Scenes Technique to help a person solve a problem, such as a health problem, a relationship problem, or a business problem. Use visualization to receive (recall) a mental image of the situation as it exists now, the problem. Then go to the second scene, to your left (towards the future in the subjective dimension), and visualize whatever you are doing to correct the problem. Then with your imagination, create and transmit to the physical dimension the desired end result, your goal, in the third scene, farthest to your left.

Use this same technique to create better health, better relationships, a better job or increased business, better grades, any traits or characteristics you desire for yourself—anything at all that you want to have, to do, or to be.

In the future, when you think of your project, visualize (recall) the goal you created with your imagination in the subjective dimension. Take it for granted that the solution already exists, and is being transmitted to the physical dimension so it can manifest there.

This is what is meant by the phrase "Pray believing you have already received." Our way of saying it is, "Program in the future in a past tense sense."

Take it for granted, and you will get your results.

You can use the same technique to help other people. When you are in a person's presence and they are in a receptive state, such as being at the alpha level, or being in a state of confusion, suspense, or anticipation, then enter your level by defocusing your vision (as you do when you are daydreaming with your eyes open) and program the person with the use of the Three Scenes Technique. First, recall (receive information) about the existing situation (the problem), then use your imagination to create a solution (goal) and transmit it to the physical dimension. Just be certain you do your programming in the subjective dimension—while at your level.

Always keep the Laws of Programming in mind, and remember that the solution must be the best for everybody concerned.

Using the Three Scenes Technique

Here are several examples of how you can use the Silva Ultra-Mind ESP Systems Three Scenes Technique for self-management:

1. When working on a health problem for yourself or someone else, enter your center with the 3 to 1 Method and use the Three Scenes Technique. Picture the problem in the first scene, directly in front of you. Make a good study of the situation by recalling details. After making a good study of the problem, erase the problem image.

   Then in a second scene, approximately 15 degrees toward your left, mentally picture the things that are being done to correct the health problem, and the corrections beginning to take place. You can include conventional medicine, holistic faith healing, nutrition, physical therapy and exercise, and anything else that is being done. If you have worked on this project before, then take into account any changes that have taken place since the last time you worked on it.

   In the third scene, approximately 15 degrees to the left of the second scene, mentally picture the person in perfect health. Mentally picture all of the benefits of this. The more people who benefit, the better.

   Remember, in health areas, consult your physician and work under medical supervision.

2. If you desire to use the Three Scenes Technique for weight control, begin by entering your center with the 3 to 1 Method and picture the problem in the first scene. You

could imagine that you are looking at yourself in a mirror. Make a good study of the problem. Notice any foods or eating habits that might be contributing to the problem.

In the second scene, 15 degrees to the left of the first scene, mentally picture what you are doing to correct the problem. This could include changes in the foods that you eat, the amount that you eat, and the way that you eat. You can picture yourself in this second scene deciding not to eat dessert or other foods that you know contribute to the problem. You can picture yourself exercising appropriately, practicing stress management techniques, or doing anything else that you have determined will help you.

In the third scene, 15 degrees to the left of the second scene, picture yourself at your ideal weight and size. Mentally picture all of the benefits of this. Remember, the more people who benefit, the better.

3. To use the Three Scenes Technique to help you stop smoking, begin by entering your center with the 3 to 1 Method, and picture the problem in the first scene. Notice when you smoke the first cigarette of the day. Notice what kind of situations cause you to desire a cigarette.

In the second scene, to the left of the first scene, picture yourself changing the habit patterns. For instance, you might picture yourself smoking the first cigarette of the day one hour later, and over time continuing to postpone the first cigarette to an even later time, until you smoke only a few cigarettes a day. At that time it will be easy to stop smoking completely.

You can picture yourself smoking only one cigarette per hour, on the hour, instead of reacting to the situations that used to cause you to desire a cigarette. Then you could picture yourself smoking one cigarette every two hours, and continue reducing the number of cigarettes you smoke until it is easy to stop smoking altogether.

In the third scene, to the left of the second scene, picture yourself as a nonsmoker, and that you will never smoke again in your life. Mentally picture all of the benefits of this. Be a good example for your children. Remember, the more people who benefit, the better.

4. If you desire to change your behavior, or to improve a skill, you can program this with the Three Scenes Technique.

In the first scene, mentally picture the activity you desire to change. If you become angry, then picture yourself the last time you lost your temper. If you experience irrational fears, then picture yourself the last time you experienced the fear. If there is a skill that you desire to improve, then picture yourself performing at your current skill level. Make a good study of the problem, by noticing the details.

Then in the second scene, to the left of the first scene, mentally picture what you are doing to change the situation. Picture yourself using anger management techniques in order to help you control your temper. If you are programming to overcome an irrational fear, then picture yourself programming to feel comfortable doing the thing that you used to fear, and imagine the desired change beginning to take place. If you want to improve the way you perform an activity, then imagine a teacher or coach showing you how to do it, and recall how it feels to do it correctly.

In the third scene, 15 degrees to the left of the second scene, picture yourself the way you desire to be: relaxed, confident, competent, and happy. Picture yourself doing the things you want to do in the way that you desire to do them. Mentally picture all of the benefits of this. Remember, the more people who benefit, the better.

Primary Perception

In 1966, around the time when José Silva was preparing to teach his very first public class, Cleve Backster connected his polygraph— "lie detector"—to a houseplant called a dragon tree to see if he could detect or measure any reactions when he watered it.

There was a very clear reaction, so he wondered what else he could do. He thought to himself, "I know what I am going to do: I am going to burn that plant leaf, that very leaf that's attached to the polygraph."

At the very moment that he had that thought, the polygraph indicated a huge reaction from the plant. Backster explained:

"I didn't have matches in the room. I wasn't touching the plant. I was five feet away from the plant. The only new thing that occurred was my intent to burn that plant leaf.

"And at that moment the polygraph went into a wild agitation.

"This was very late at night. The building was empty, and there was just no other reason for this reaction. I thought, 'Wow! This thing read my mind!' It was that obvious to me right then.

This, I would say, would be a very high-quality observation, and my consciousness hasn't been the same since."

Cleve Backster continued to conduct research into what he called *primary perception*. He learned many things.

In the first place, pretending doesn't work. "There is a difference between *pretend* and *intend*," he said. Scientists who sit and think about burning a plant without actually intending to burn the plant do not get the same reaction.

In the second place, primary perception extends to the cell level. Backster has conducted numerous experiments with white blood cells from human beings. They react to your thoughts and emotions, providing further scientific evidence that your thoughts and your body's radiation affect everything and everybody around you.

Preconditioning Projection into Tree and Leaves

In your next mental projection exercise, you will first project to a tree and study the tree through a full growing season. Select a fruit tree that blossoms before bearing fruit, a citrus tree for instance. You will study it first when it only has blossoms. Then, after the blossoms fall off, you will study the small, unripened fruit. Then you will study the fully grown fruit.

Next you will project into two leaves. To prepare for this, we want you to go and pick two leaves, one from each of two different species of plant.

Study these two leaves prior to the exercise, the same way you studied the metals in the previous exercise. After you study them, bring them to your forehead, one at a time. Touch your forehead with the leaf, close your eyes, and make an impression.

During the conditioning cycle, you will review your objective impressions to transfer the objective impressions to your right brain hemisphere, and then you will use mental projection to project into each leaf and establish subjective points of reference.

Remember to use your hands. This will produce a more vivid experience for you.

Remember that we do not wait passively to *perceive* something; we *project* in order to achieve the most effective experience.

When you are ready, and have made objective impressions of the two leaves, then continue with the exercise below.

Projection into Tree and Leaves

We will now continue programming Effective Sensory Projection for your success, and will program information with the use of mental projection for your benefit. We will establish subjective points of reference by projecting into the kingdom of animate matter and into the plant kingdom, becoming aware of different levels and different depths. Our present project is projection to a fruit tree during seasonal changes, and a study of the leaves and fruit.

At this time, project yourself mentally to be standing next to a fruit tree that blossoms before bearing fruit. You are now standing right next to a fruit tree that has only leaves.

Now you will objectively extend your arm and reach out to cut off a leaf. Objectively extend your arm, reach out and cut off a leaf. (pause) Now mentally crush this leaf with your fingers; (pause) bring it to your nostrils, and mentally impress the odor. (pause) Whatever you perceive with your imagination at this dimension you can use as a point of reference in the future.

Time is moving on; (pause) blossoms are beginning to appear; (pause) the tree is now in full bloom. Now objectively reach out and cut off a blossom. (pause) Crush it with your fingers, (pause) bring it to your nostrils, and mentally make an impression. (pause) Whatever you perceive with your imagination at this dimension you can use as a point of reference in the future.

Time is moving on; (pause) blossoms are falling off; (pause) the tree now has very small, unripened fruit. (pause) Now reach out and cut off a small, unripened fruit; (pause) crush it with your fingers; (pause) bring it to your nostrils, and mentally make an impression. (pause) Whatever you perceive with your imagination at this dimension you can use as a point of reference in the future.

Time is moving on; (pause) the fruit is growing; (pause) it is now fully grown but unripened. (pause) Now reach out and cut off a fully grown unripened fruit. (pause) Break the skin, (pause) bring it to your nostrils, and mentally make an impression. (pause) Whatever you perceive with your imagination at this dimension you can use as a point of reference in the future.

Time is moving on; (pause) the fruit is ripening; (pause) it is now ripe. (pause) Now reach out and cut off a ripened fruit, (pause) break the skin, (pause) bring it to your nostrils, and mentally make an impression. (pause) Whatever you perceive with your imagination at this dimension you can use as a point of reference in the future.

Now the tree will disappear, and you will mentally project yourself to your living room. (pause) Mentally project yourself to the center of your living room, facing the south wall. You are now at the center of your living room, facing the south wall.

We will now replay the objective impressions of the leaves and will also establish subjective points of reference. Now we will visualize the first leaf. Extend your arm objectively and visualize the first leaf. Mentally sense the leaf. (pause) Bring it closer and closer to your forehead. (pause) Now touch your forehead and mentally project yourself into the leaf. (pause) You are now within the first leaf. You may return your hand to rest on your lap.

Now test for light. Sense the intensity and color of light within the leaf. (pause) How does light within the leaf compare with the light within aluminum, (pause) brass, (pause) copper, (pause) and stainless steel? (pause) Whatever you perceive with your imagination at this dimension you can use as a point of reference in the future.

Now test for temperature. Sense the temperature within the leaf. (pause) How does this compare with the temperature of aluminum, (pause) brass, (pause) copper, (pause) and stainless steel? (pause) Whatever you perceive with your imagination at this dimension you can use as a point of reference in the future.

Now test for odor. Sense the odor within the leaf. (pause) How does this compare with the odor of aluminum, (pause) brass, (pause) copper, (pause) and stainless steel? (pause) Whatever you perceive with your imagination at this dimension you can use as a point of reference in the future.

Now test for solidity of material. Objectively form a fist and knock on the inside of the leaf. (pause) How does this reflected sound compare with the reflected sound of aluminum, (pause) brass, (pause) copper, (pause) and stainless steel? (pause) Whatever you perceive with your imagination at this dimension you can use as a point of reference in the future.

Now touch your forehead to come out of the leaf. (pause) You are now coming out of the leaf. Extend your arm and mentally hold the leaf at arm's length. Now allow the leaf to float in space, using the south wall of your living room as a background. Keep the leaf rotating. You may return your hand to rest on your lap. (pause)

Now the color of the wall will change to red. (pause) How does the leaf stand out against a red background? (pause) How does this compare with aluminum, (pause) brass, (pause) copper, (pause) and stainless steel? (pause) Keep the leaf rotating. (pause)

Now the color of the wall will change to green. (pause) How does the leaf stand out against a green background? (pause) How does this compare with aluminum, (pause) brass, (pause) copper, (pause) and stainless steel? (pause) Keep the leaf rotating.

Now the color of the wall will change to blue. (pause) How does the leaf stand out against a blue background? (pause) How does this compare with aluminum, (pause) brass, (pause) copper, (pause) and stainless steel? (pause) Keep the leaf rotating.

Now the color of the wall will change back to green (snap fingers), back to red, (snap fingers) back to the actual color of the wall. (snap fingers) Now the first leaf will disappear from the scene. (snap fingers) The first leaf has disappeared from the scene.

Now we will visualize the second leaf. (pause) Extend your arm objectively and visualize the second leaf. Mentally sense this leaf as you bring it closer and closer toward your forehead. (pause) Now touch your forehead and mentally project yourself into the leaf. (pause) You are now within the leaf. You may return your hand to rest on your lap.

Now test for light. (pause) Sense the intensity and color of the light within this second leaf. (pause) How does the light within this

leaf compare with the light within the first leaf? (pause) Whatever
you perceive with your imagination at this dimension, you can use
as a point of reference in the future.

At the count of 3, test for temperature. 1 – 2 – 3. (snap fingers)
Sense the temperature within this leaf. (pause) How does it compare with the temperature within the first leaf? (pause) Whatever
you perceive with your imagination at this dimension you can use
as a point of reference in the future.

Now test for odor. (pause) Sense the odor within this same
leaf. (pause) How does this compare with the odor of the other
leaf? (pause) Whatever you perceive with your imagination at this
dimension you can use as a point of reference in the future.

Now test for solidity of material. (pause) Objectively form a fist
and knock on the inside of this second leaf. (pause) How does this
sound compare with the sound of the first leaf? (pause) Whatever
you perceive with your imagination at this dimension you can use
as a point of reference in the future.

Now touch your forehead and come out of the leaf. (pause)
Touch your forehead; you are now coming out of the leaf. Extend
your arm and mentally hold the leaf at arm's length, allowing it to
float in space against the background of your south wall. Keep the
leaf rotating. You may return your hand to rest on your lap. (pause)

Now the color of the wall will change to red. (pause) How
does the second leaf stand out against a red background? (pause)
How does this compare with the first leaf? Keep the second leaf
rotating. (pause)

Now the color of the wall will change to green. (pause) How
does the leaf stand out against a green background? (pause) How
does this compare with the first leaf? Keep the second leaf rotating. (pause)

Now the color of the wall will change to blue. (now) How does the leaf stand out against a blue background? (pause) How does this compare with the first leaf? Keep the second leaf rotating. (pause)

The color of the wall will now change back to green, (pause) back to red, (pause) back to the actual color of the wall (pause). The second leaf will now disappear from the scene. (pause) The second leaf has now disappeared. Whatever you perceive with your imagination at this dimension you can use as points of reference in the future.

It is now an accomplished fact that subjective points of reference have been established in the animate matter kingdom with reproductive intelligence—the plant-life kingdom—at different levels and different depths. To function at these levels and to use these points of reference, all you need is a sincere desire to solve problems. Your mind will automatically seek out these points of reference where you will perceive and become aware of information you can use to solve such problems. And this is so.

You have practiced entering deep, healthy levels of mind. In your next session, you will enter a deeper, healthier level of mind, faster and easier than this time.

Now, when you are ready, count yourself out of your level. Take your time.

Tips on How to Proceed

Remember to continue to practice the Silva Centering Exercise. We recommend practicing it between each of these mental projection exercises, the same as we do in the live seminars:

✗ Silva Centering Exercise

✗ Projection to Home

✗ Silva Centering Exercise

✗ Projection into Inanimate Matter Kingdom

✗ Silva Centering Exercise

✗ Projection into Plant Life Kingdom

__ Silva Centering Exercise

__ Projection into Animate Matter Kingdom

__ Silva Centering Exercise

__ Projection into Human Kingdom

After you have completed the training, you can maintain your ability by using what you have learned to solve problems. We recommend that you go to the alpha level at least once a day, for five minutes. Twice a day is better; three times a day is excellent.

To practice for five minutes each time is good, 10 minutes is better, 15 minutes is excellent.

6

Your Private Tutor

If you are like me, you have probably wondered about some of the great questions of life, such as: Where did we come from? Where are we going? What is my purpose while I am here?

José Silva wondered about those things. "If God is all-powerful, then why was I created?" he wondered. Then his insight into the mind—which is not physical—and the body—which is—provided an answer:

"I was created to correct problems in the physical dimension," he reasoned. "You are to God like your fingers are to your hand," he explained.

Mr. Silva told us what our purpose in life is. That purpose is to correct problems, to relieve suffering, improve living conditions, and convert the planet into a paradise.

A lot of people seem to equate "purpose in life" with something that will make them happy, or something that will at least bring them a sense of satisfaction.

Mr. Silva said that we were not sent here for a vacation; we were not sent here for an 80-year coffee break. We were sent here to work, to improve conditions on the planet and complete the creation. We are co-creators, he said. We can do here on planet earth what higher intelligence can do throughout the entire universe.

So the only question would be how to go about fulfilling our mission.

That isn't difficult to figure out. Just look around. What problems do you see, and what can you do to correct them?

Mr. Silva lived his entire life that way.

It was this attitude that led him to begin his research. He began to study psychology on his own when he was a 30-year-old father, because he wanted to find ways to help his children make better grades and be more successful in life.

His research expanded far beyond anything he anticipated, because of his attitude that he would help anybody who needed help. When people saw how well his children were doing, they began asking him to help their children, and eventually the adults wanted to learn the techniques themselves.

He didn't do it for money. In fact, for 22 years he paid for all of his own research. He never even let anybody reimburse him for gasoline, or bridge tolls, or any other expenses. He was earning a good living with his electronics repair business, and he felt that there was probably a relationship there. He believed that higher intelligence provided him with the means to earn enough money to conduct the research.

Many years later, when the Silva Mind Control course was being taught in more than 100 countries in two dozen different languages, and people all over the world were thanking him for showing them how to change their lives for the better, he confirmed what you might suspect: if he had known in the beginning what he was getting himself into and how much opposition he would face and how hard this would be on him and his family, he would have just continued with electronics repair and not done the research.

Instead he followed the guidance that he got. A couple of times he decided he had learned enough and it was time to end his research, and he received indications from higher intelligence that they wanted him to continue. So he did. "Not my will, but Thy will be done—"Thy will" being the will of higher intelligence.

Back in 1973 he told a group of scientists that he knew he didn't create the Silva Method on his own. He told them, "We ourselves cannot explain . . . the success that we have had, except through help from higher levels. And that is putting it lightly."

He went on to tell the scientists that that was the next thing he wanted to research. "Can we establish a better communication with higher levels of intelligence, wherever they are?"

He found the answer in 1997 with the MentalVideo technique.

The MentalVideo

Here is the formula for the MentalVideo technique:

Whenever you need to use the MentalVideo, proceed in the following manner: At beta, with your eyes open, mentally create, with visualization, a MentalVideo of a problem, or the existing situation. Include everything that belongs to the animate matter kingdom. *Animate matter* means everything that contains life.

After you have completed the MentalVideo of the problem, use visualization to review it at beta, with your eyes closed.

Later, when you are in bed and ready to go to sleep, go to your center with the 3 to 1 Method. Once you are at your center, review the MentalVideo that you created of the problem earlier when you were at beta.

After you have reviewed the problem, mentally convert the problem into a project. Then create, with imagination, a Mental-Video of the solution.

The MentalVideo of the solution should contain a step-by-step procedure of how you desire the project to be resolved.

After both of the MentalVideos have been completed, go to sleep with the intention of delivering the MentalVideos to your tutor while you sleep. Take for granted that the delivery will be made.

During the next three days, look for indications that point to the solution. Every time you think of the project, think of the solution that you created in the MentalVideo, in the past tense.

You can imagine creating the videos any way you like. You can imagine hiring a crew from a local television station, or you can imagine using your smartphone to record the videos.

You can use short clips to depict the situation, like on the local television news. They have a very short time to tell a story, so they make each video clip count. You can do the same with your MentalVideos.

Just send enough information for higher intelligence to get the picture of the problem, and your proposed solution.

You can imagine delivering the videos any way you like: in an overnight pouch or through a superfast wireless network.

Solving Problems with the MentalVideo

It is very simple to use the MentalVideo. At night, when you are ready to go to sleep, you first create a mental video of the problem, such as: a machine that is not working, a response not arriving from overseas, a glitch in a computer system that is proving difficult to correct.

During the next three days, look for indications of how to proceed:

A most unlikely person comes up with an ingenious substitute for a missing part.

A "lost" shipment shows up the next morning.

A stranger appears with exactly what is needed.

A flash of insight permits you to take a totally new tack or approach that turns out to be successful.

All we can say is "coincidence."

José Silva's definition of coincidence is: "God's way of showing his hand."

Make sure when you do your MentalVideos that you let your needs be known, plus a little bit more. That was Mr. Silva's advice. He explained: "Do not ask for more than you need, but do ask for no less than what you need."

There is plenty of work that needs to be done. Our job is to do the work, whether we want to do it or not. Just look around and see what needs to be done, and get to work. Report to your mentor with the MentalVideo technique, seek guidance, seek help when you need it, and you will receive it. Keep in mind what your needs are, plus a little bit more, and all your needs will be taken care of too.

Mr. Silva's favorite formula addresses this:

"Seek ye first the kingdom of heaven." We think this means the alpha level.

"Function within God's righteousness." Do what God sent you here to do.

"And all else shall be added unto you."

Notice that the formula doesn't say that we should share some of our good fortune with others *after* our needs are met. It doesn't work that way. How many people have a job where they get paid first, and then they are supposed to go do the work? Not many. We are compensated for what we do.

The Correct Use for the MentalVideo

The MentalVideo is a communications tool that you can use to communicate with the hierarchy of intelligences that reign over the universe. That is how Mr. Silva explained it. So you don't actually use it to program yourself. You use it to obtain guidance so that you can make the correct decisions and do what higher intelligence sent you here to do.

The Three Scenes Technique that we covered in the previous chapter is the correct tool for us to use to do our work.

The MentalVideo is for sending messages back to headquarters to report on our progress, and obtain guidance—to make sure we are doing what is best—and to request reinforcements to help us correct problems and improve living conditions.

Since we are communicating between the objective dimension and the subjective dimension, everything has to be converted into a different form.

We use visualization and imagination—the MentalVideos—to send information, and we receive our guidance and help in a way that we can confirm and verify: "coincidences" in the physical world.

When you can "see" the answer from higher intelligence with your own eyes—and can confirm it if necessary—then you can be confident that you are being guided by higher intelligence—by God. Objective feedback and repeatability make the technique scientifically valid, and remove all doubt about whether you are doing the right thing.

We have to be partners in the process. We cannot just turn it over to higher intelligence, any more than we can try to do it all on our own.

If you hired an expert at Internet marketing to set up a website for you, and they came and told you to give them all the copy you wanted on the website, and copies of all the art you wanted to use, and to show them how you wanted it laid out, you'd thank them politely (I hope) and tell them you no longer needed their services.

On the other hand, if you hired somebody and they went to work, but never asked you about your business and your business goals, never showed you what they were doing, never consulted with you, then, when the website was completed, it might not be of any use to you.

It is the same with higher intelligence. It is always a partnership. We need to do our work and make our best guess. Then, in order to be sure we are doing the right thing, we need to submit our plans to higher intelligence—including how we plan to carry them out.

How to Find Your Right Work

There are people who don't know what kind of work they should be doing. They can't just put in a request and expect higher intelligence to figure it all out for them. "It is not our job to put God to work. God sent us here to do the work," José Silva said.

We suggest to those people that they go to their level and think about what they enjoyed doing when they were young, what their hopes and dreams were, what people said they were good at. Also think about what is needed in the world, what kind of work needs to be done. When you do all of that, you can get some ideas. You might not hit on the right one, but at least it gives higher intelligence something to work with.

Someone once asked Ed Bernd about the phrase in the Bible, "The meek shall inherit the earth." He didn't have an explanation at the time. But then one night, while thinking about the Ultra-Mind ESP System and the MentalVideo, an idea came to him. Here is his explanation:

We had never thought of José Silva as "meek." He was a fighter who would defend his work against anybody. Nobody pushed him around. But a thought "came to me" that night, so I did what Mr. Silva used to do and got out my dictionary and looked up the word "meek."

The definition was "easily imposed upon" and "submissive to the will of others."

Definitely not José Silva, right?

Unless you complete these phrases this way:

"Easily imposed upon by higher intelligence.

"Submissive to the will of God."

He wanted to quit doing his research more than once. He was being told by everybody that he should quit—everybody except higher intelligence. He submitted to the will of higher intelligence.

Now we know how to get the kind of guidance he got, and to get it on a more regular basis. We are in a better position than he was to do this now that he has given us the MentalVideo Technique.

Using the MentalVideo

Here is how Ed uses the MentalVideo.

My understanding is that we need to do the legwork and come up with a plan, and we need to keep the boss—higher intelligence—advised of what we are doing. Then keep looking for guidance (the dictionary defines *look* as "to use your physical eyesight") and then follow the guidance.

The way I do it is to say, "This is my plan and this is what I am going to do unless you tell me otherwise."

If they want me to alter my plans, or to stop and do something entirely different, they know how to let me know by the "indications" or "coincidences" that steer me in the right direction.

If I don't get any indications to change, then I take that to mean that I am on the right track and to keep going full speed ahead.

Why Some People Seem to Be So Lucky

Have you ever noticed that some people seem to have "lucky coincidences" happen to them frequently? It is because they function naturally at the alpha level, and probably have also used the principles of the MentalVideo without knowing it.

Sam Gonzalez Silva observed this in his own life. He used to tell students that if you intended to program for someone before going to sleep at night, and you fell asleep before you completed the programming, it would still work anyway. We'll let him explain exactly what happened:

How I found out that I was still effective with my programing even after I fell asleep was that while I was director of the Mental Health Crisis Unit, a nurse on my staff approached me and asked if I could help her with her back, which had been acting up, and she had been in pain for the past two days. She was aware that I helped others with their aches and pains and asked if I would help her out. She was working swing shift at that time.

That evening when I went to bed, around midnight, I had other projects to work on, and I decided to leave her for last so that I would send her good, strong, lasting healing energy. Before I knew it and after working my other cases, it was morning and I realized I had not worked her case.

When I went to work that morning, I was feeling very embarrassed and really bad because I had not worked her case. At one point I even thought of leaving early, before she got to work, so that I would not face her and let her know that I had done nothing to help her.

To my surprise, when she got to work she came into my office and very excitedly informed me that she could tell exactly when I worked her case.

She told me that when she got off at 11:30 p.m. she went straight home, and when she got there her husband was up and they talked for a while. She talked to him about the severe pain in her back and how she was hoping that she would be able to sleep. Then she decided to go to bed and try to get some sleep. She said that after lying in bed for a few minutes, she felt her back start to radiate with heat, and her pain went away.

After this incident, I started to think about other cases in the past when I had intended to work the cases but fell asleep first, and I had the same results: I was effective with my casework.

The authors have seen this happen with many Silva students, and also in their own lives. There are two possible explanations:

When you have worked a lot of cases, as Sam has done, then you begin to use the alpha level naturally, just like the 10 percent of people who are natural alpha thinkers. José Silva explained that your brain dips into alpha approximately 30 times every minute, for very short periods—just microseconds. With practice, you can extend that time, and learn to use it to solve problems. We explain how in chapter 8.

When José Silva developed the MentalVideo technique, another possibility occurred to us. He always told us that the doorway to the "other side"—the spiritual dimension where higher intelligence resides—is at the very low delta brain-wave frequencies.

When you go to sleep with images of the problem and the solution in mind, there is a possibility that higher intelligence will get the message and send you some help in the form of "coincidences."

Now, with the MentalVideo, you can ask for help from higher intelligence whenever you need it, even if you haven't developed proficiency in using the alpha level yet.

All you need in order for the MentalVideo to work for you, José Silva told us, is to follow the formula, have a sincere desire to solve the problem, and go to sleep. If you comply with the Laws of Programming, and you are willing to allow higher intelligence to work through you, you will succeed.

How to Make Sure That God Is on Your Side

Higher intelligence—God—will join you in your efforts—when you are doing what God wants done.

God didn't create us so he could do *our* bidding. We were created to do what God wants done. It is through us that God has a presence on planet earth, in the physical dimension.

When your plans are to improve living conditions on planet earth, then higher intelligence will help you make the correct decisions and get it right the first time.

Ms. Xue Kuiyang, whose English name is Sunflower, directs our Silva UltraMind operations in Beijing, China. She has some excellent examples of how higher intelligence can guide you to success when your efforts will improve life here on earth. Here's what she had to say:

> One of my Silva graduates runs an education company that specialized in training teenagers to becoming future leaders in different fields like politics, education, sales, business, health, and so on. There are many opportunities, and he wanted to be sure to choose the right partners and to proceed in the best possible way.
>
> To help him in his decision making process, he thought of his company's products and services as the "chain," other related products and services as "pearls," and made a "necklace" for his education system.

In order to succeed, he needed to attract the right partner to the right position in each part of the necklace. He did a lot of work, and wanted to be sure that he made the correct decisions about each of the partners and how they would fit into the system.

I used the MentalVideo technique to present the project to higher intelligence. My first video included the work he had already done and the decisions he needed to make for connecting the education company with potential cooperation partners from their mission perspective.

When we view the project from a life mission perspective—that we were sent here to solve problems and improve living conditions—we become one and harmonious. We each do what we do best, and what will provide the most value, with the attitude that the best thing will be done for everybody concerned.

On the morning of the second day after I sent the MentalVideo, a mission-oriented solution came to me: to build up a platform for project-related partners to work together and distribute the benefits and profits properly and encouragingly.

Once he had a clear idea of exactly how to proceed, he knew exactly what to say to his potential partners. He knew how to negotiate with them, and was able to show them how to contribute their products and services to his education company and sell them to teenagers and their parents in the most cost-effective way.

We did not force things to be done our way. We studied every aspect of the business and then followed the guidance from higher intelligence.

It is always nice when a project comes together smoothly and is a big success. The big question is: will the same approach work again? If this is a scientifically valid approach to obtaining guidance and help from higher intelligence, then we should be able to use it reliably, and see objective results from it.

Here is a recent example of how Sunflower made faster progress on a project than she had expected, when she used the MentalVideo:

After teaching the Silva UltraMind ESP System in China for nearly eleven years, I decided to write a book based on my working experience in teaching foreign doctors to learn traditional Chinese medicine, including acupuncture, massage, Taiji, and Qigong. My working title is Xue's Taiji Zen.

When I discussed the project with my publisher, they asked me about how to sell and use the book. I told them that I preferred to offer it to the Taiji Zen company. Taiji Zen is a lifestyle company founded by Jet Li and Jack Ma with the mission of spreading "Health and Happiness for All" through a balance of physical wellness and mental fitness—the Taiji Zen lifestyle.

I think that my Taiji Zen is a merging of the oriental wisdom and western science. But it is not easy at all to get a meeting with the president of their Taiji Zen company.

So I used the MentalVideo technique to ask higher intelligence to help. Three days later I met one of my Silva graduates and discussed how he could use intuition to help his business. During the meeting I told him about my plan to write the Taiji Zen book.

He replied that the president of the Taiji Zen company wanted to meet him the coming week. So he invited me to go with him to the meeting.

I met with both the president and the sales manager of the Taiji Zen company. I worked health case on the sales manager before my second meeting with her, and programmed for her continued good health. We had a good talk and discussed the various ways we can cooperate, for a win-win goal.

I was surprised and excited that my dream came true so fast. Thank higher intelligence for arranging the coincidence.

MentalVideo Helps Him Land His Dream Job

Another Silva UltraMind ESP Systems graduate, Raj Ayyar, used the MentalVideo technique to help him get his dream job teaching philosophy and humanities to college students.

"Thanks to the regular use of Silva programming techniques, especially the MentalVideo and the Three Scenes techniques," he wrote us three years ago, "I have manifested a full-time teaching position, teaching philosophy and humanities at a prestigious tech university in New Delhi, India! A small miracle, since it challenges all the consensus reality odds against someone age sixty-three landing a full-time academic position."

Raj added, "I feel grateful and yet a wee bit anxious going back to full-time teaching after a decade or more," even though, he said, "I have taught part-time for many years, in addition to my full-time job." With the help of the Silva techniques, everything worked out for him.

Just as we were finishing up this book, we heard from him with this great news: "My contract at the tech university has been extended for a fourth year in a row!"

Guidance from a Natural Alpha Thinker

Just a few months after José Silva's passing, we came across a book by a natural alpha thinker who had a special gift for explaining what he did. Anyone who can function at the alpha level can benefit from his writings. The author is Robert Collier (1885–1950), and many of his books are still available from his family.

There is a paragraph in Collier's book *Riches within Your Reach: The Law of the Higher Potential*, published in 1947, just three years before his death, that answers a question that many Silva graduates have asked over the years: "Why is it when I have a really strong desire for something, and I really need it, and it will benefit many people, and I program really hard for it, I still don't get results? I get great results on little things that are not so important; why not this?"

Collier's guidance expresses one of the main principles that my father incorporated into the UltraMind ESP System: we do all that we can to fulfill the plan that higher intelligence has for us.

Here is the way Collier said it:

Look at the first chapter of the Scriptures. When God wanted light, did He strive and struggle, trying to make light? No, He said—"Let there be light."

When you want something very much, instead of trying to make it come your way, suppose you try asking for it and then letting it come. Suppose you just relax, and let God work through you instead of trying to make Him do something for you. Suppose you say to yourself, "I will do whatever is given me to do. I will follow every lead to the best of my ability, but for the rest, it is all up to the God in me. God in me knows what

my right work is, where it is, and just what I should do to get it.
I put myself and my affairs lovingly in His hands, secure that
whatever is for my highest good, He will bring to me."

Being Fired Opens Up New Opportunity

Higher intelligence knows what your right work is, and can guide
you to it if you are willing to submit to its will and follow its guidance.

A man attending one of José Silva's classes programmed to get
a promotion. Mr. Silva had explained how to use the Best Time to
Program technique to wake up automatically and program. (We
will explain the Best Time to Program technique in chapter 9.) This
was many years before he developed the MentalVideo technique,
but it had the same main elements. The man used visualization,
and went to sleep immediately after doing the programming.

He didn't get the results he asked for. He got fired.

He was very angry when he called José Silva and told him about
this. Mr. Silva told him to have faith and keep programming.

A few days later the man called again, happy this time, because
he had gotten a call from another company offering him an even
better job than he had programmed for. This company wouldn't
have offered him a job otherwise, because they were competitors
with the company that had just fired him, and they felt it would
be unethical to try to hire him away from the company he was
working for.

Whole-Brain Functioning Becomes Natural

All of the techniques you learn in the Silva UltraMind ESP System
will begin to happen naturally, without your even noticing, once

you have practiced and used them enough and gained enough confidence in them.

When you first learn something new, you have to think about how to do it. As you continue to use it, it becomes natural. If you have ever learned to ride a bicycle, you know exactly what we mean.

At first it requires all of your attention as you struggle to keep your balance, telling people, "Stay away, let me go, I've got it!"

Who Is Your Tutor?

José Silva believed that the universe is much too large and complex to be governed by just one single entity. He felt that higher intelligence—God—would have many helpers. Here is how he explained it:

> When people refer to God, as in "God helps me," we believe that this refers to a supervisor in a system. This system has been established to take care of you while you are functioning within the physical universe.
>
> This system would have to include many God helpers, or smaller gods, or angels.
>
> It would seem that it has to be this way, for expecting a single being at the top, a God, to handle everything would be like expecting the leader of a nation to handle every detail personally.
>
> Governments are composed of vast numbers of people who each perform tasks, and who each report to someone higher than they are, all the way up to the person in charge at the top. Businesses are structured the same way. Surely the intelligence

that governs the universe must be intelligent enough to build a system along the same lines. In fact, that's probably where we got the idea to use that kind of structure for business and governments.

When you get help from an agency of the government, you are getting help from the government. You don't need to go to the leader of a country in order to get a burned-out streetlight replaced. You go to a representative of the government who is assigned to do that.

When you get help from any entity that helps the Godly hierarchy or intelligence to take care of life in the universe, you are getting help from God. You are getting help from an entity that is connected to some level on the hierarchy of intelligence.

Intelligence is God, and any time we use intelligence, we are using God. In other words, it takes intelligence to solve problems; it takes human intelligence to solve problems.

Your tutor is your own personal representative in the hierarchy of intelligences that we refer to as *higher intelligence*.

Your tutor can communicate with my tutor and anyone else's tutor in order to arrange "coincidences" to help us correct problems and improve living conditions on earth.

The Soul Mold

Remember that you cannot cause a problem with your mind at a distance. The subjective dimension is an "attractive" dimension—it attracts matter to conform to the blueprint that nature intended. Mr. Silva referred to this blueprint of perfection as the *soul mold*.

Since this is such a new science, and he was discovering things that had never been imagined before, he had to create some new terminology and sometimes apply new definitions to old words. Here is how he defined *soul*:

The soul is a mold that holds matter together. It is cohesive and adhesive.

Religious people think of the soul as the spiritual part of the human being. José Silva used the term *human intelligence* for the spiritual part of a human being, and he used the term *biological intelligence* for the programming of the physical body of the human being.

In the physical dimension, we use *repulsion* to correct problems. If we make a mistake while doing this, we could cause a problem. You can cause problems in the physical dimension by using force.

In the subjective dimension, we use *attraction* to correct problems. You cannot use mental images to attract matter to do something it doesn't want to do.

The physical body wants to conform to the soul mold; you cannot attract it away from the natural perfection that nature intended. Only some kind of physical force can push it away from its natural state.

This means that your thoughts cannot hurt anybody as long as they are beyond the range of the physical part of your aura. Because your mind cannot hurt anyone at a distance, it is all right to project the idea of problems in order to help you mentally detect whether or not your subject has any of these problems.

Remember to use your hands; this will produce a more vivid experience for you.

Remember that we do not wait passively to *perceive* something, we *project* in order to achieve the most effective experience.

Studying the Anatomy of a Pet

We will continue programming Effective Sensory Projection for your success, and will continue programming information with the use of mental projection for your benefit. We will establish subjective points of reference in the animate matter kingdom with reproductive intelligence—the animal life kingdom—at different levels and depths. We will study the anatomy of a pet.

Mr. Silva's intent is to use a typical house pet like a dog or cat. Remember, we study various organs, so it should be a pet that has a liver, kidneys, and similar organs.

It should be a pet that you are familiar with, so that you will already have objective impressions of the animal. Then during the conditioning cycle, you will review your objective impressions, and will then use mental projection to establish subjective points of reference.

Ideally the pet should be healthy, so that you can establish points of reference for healthy organs. If you detect anything that you suspect could be a problem, you should correct it before coming out of level.

At this time, mentally project yourself to the center of your living room facing the south wall. (pause) You are now standing at the center of your living room, facing the south wall.

Now mentally project your pet onto your mental screen. (pause) Now mentally move your pet in front of your mental screen, which is black and is used as a background. (pause) Your pet is facing you; notice how the pet stands out against the black screen. (pause) Mentally turn your pet to the left; (pause) turn the pet away from you; (pause) turn the pet to the right; (pause) place the pet facing you. (pause)

Now the color of the screen will change to red. (pause) The screen is now red. Study your pet; how does the pet stand out against a red background? (pause) Now the color of the screen will change to green. (pause) Study the pet against a green background. (pause) Now the color of the screen will change to blue. (pause) Now study the pet against a blue background. (pause) Whatever you perceive with your imagination at this dimension you can use as a point of reference in the future.

The color of your mental screen will now change back to green, (pause) back to red, (pause) back to black. (pause)

Now mentally bring your pet closer, close enough to touch, noticing how the pet appears to become bigger as it gets closer. (pause) Now objectively extend your arms and hold the pet by the head, one hand on each side. (pause) Study the head from several angles from this outer point of view. Whatever you perceive with your imagination at this dimension you can use as a point of reference in the future.

Observe the eyes, (pause) the nose, (pause) the ears, (pause) the fur or outer covering. (pause) Focus your attention on the pet's forehead. (pause) Now we will mentally enter the bone-structure level of this kingdom. (pause) We are now at the bone-structure level. Desire to perceive and imagine a bone or bones. (pause) Bring back a memory of when you have seen a skull. (pause) Study the pet's skull from several angles. (pause) Whatever you perceive with your imagination at this dimension you can use as a point of reference in the future.

Focus your attention on the pet's forehead. (pause) Now we will enter the brain-cell level. (pause) Desire to perceive and imagine brain cells or brain matter. (pause) Bring back a memory of when you have seen a brain in a picture or on a chart. (pause) Study the brain from several angles. (pause) Whatever you perceive with your imagination at this dimension you can use as a point of reference in the future.

Now we will go back to the bone-structure level. (pause) Now we will again be at the outer level of this kingdom. (pause) We are now at the outer level of this kingdom. Again observe the eyes, the nose, the ears, the fur or outer covering.

Now mentally move the pet a little higher and hold it by the rib cage; objectively place one hand on each side of the rib cage. (pause) Now focus your attention on the center of the pet's chest. (pause) Now we will enter the bone-structure level. (pause) Desire to perceive and imagine the ribs of your pet; (pause) now the spinal column; (pause) study the complete skeletal body. (pause) You can raise or lower the skeleton to any position or angle, and it will remain in that position or angle. (pause) Whatever you perceive with your imagination at this dimension you can use as a point of reference in the future.

Now focus your attention on the chest. (pause) Now we will enter the heart-tissue level. (pause) Desire to perceive and imagine a heart. (pause) Bring back a memory of when you have seen a heart. (pause) Study the heart from several angles. (pause) Whatever you perceive with your imagination at this dimension you can use as a point of reference in the future.

Again focus your attention on the heart. (pause) Now we will sense the heart as transparent. (pause) Bring back a memory of having seen a picture of a transparent heart; imagine what it would look like. (pause) Whatever you perceive with your imagination at this dimension you can use as a point of reference in the future.

Now we will enter the lung-tissue level. (pause) Desire to perceive and imagine two lungs. (pause) Bring back a memory of when you have seen pictures of lungs. (pause) Study the lungs of this pet from several angles. (pause) Whatever you perceive with your imagination at this dimension you can use as a point of reference in the future.

Now we will enter the kidney-tissue level. (pause) Desire to perceive and imagine two kidneys. (pause) Bring back a memory of having seen kidneys, such as in anatomy book pictures, or at the meat market. (pause) Study your pet's kidneys from several angles. (pause) Whatever you perceive with your imagination at this dimension you can use as a point of reference in the future.

Now we will enter the liver-tissue level. (pause) Desire to perceive and imagine a liver. (pause) Study your pet's liver from several angles. (pause) Whatever you perceive with your imagination at this dimension, you can use as a point of reference in the future.

Now we will go back to the kidney level. (pause) Now back to the lung level, (pause) now back to the heart level, (pause) now back to the skeletal level, (pause) now to the outer level of this dimension. (pause) Now mentally place your pet in front of your mental screen; (pause) now mentally turn your pet to your left; (pause) now turn it away from you; (pause) now to your right; (pause) now towards you. (pause) Change the color of the screen to red. (pause) Change the color of the screen to green. (pause) Now change the color to blue. (pause)

We will change the color of the screen back to green, (pause) back to red, (pause), back to black. (pause) Now imagine your pet in perfect health. (pause) Now cause your pet to disappear from the scene. (pause) Your pet has now disappeared from the scene.

Whatever you perceive with your imagination at this dimension you can use as points of reference in the future.

It is now an accomplished fact that subjective points of reference have been established at different levels and depths of the animate matter kingdom with reproductive intelligence—the animal-life kingdom. To function at these levels and to use these points of reference, all you need is a sincere desire to solve problems. Your mind will automatically seek out these points of reference, where you will perceive and become aware of information that you can use to solve such problems. And this is so.

You have practiced entering deep, healthy levels of mind. In your next session, you will enter a deeper, healthier level of mind, faster and easier than this time.

Now when you are ready, count yourself out of your level. Take your time.

Tips on How to Proceed

Remember: if you record these instructions and listen to the recording, or if you have someone read them to you, then you can do the entire exercise—all four segments—in one session.

If you are memorizing what to do and then are doing it on your own without anybody guiding you, it will be easier to do the exercise one segment at a time.

Also remember to continue to practice the Silva Centering Exercise. We recommend practicing it between each of these mental projection exercises, the same as we do in the live seminars:

X Silva Centering Exercise

X Projection to Home

X Silva Centering Exercise

X Projection into Inanimate Matter Kingdom

✗ Silva Centering Exercise
✗ Projection into Plant Life Kingdom
✗ Silva Centering Exercise
✗ Projection into Animate Matter Kingdom
__ Silva Centering Exercise
__ Projection into Human Kingdom

After you have completed the training, then you can maintain your ability by using what you have learned to solve problems. We recommend that you go to the alpha level at least once a day, for five minutes. Twice a day is better, three times a day is excellent.

To practice for five minutes each time is good, 10 minutes is better, 15 minutes is excellent.

7

ESP Demystified

As we mentioned previously, ESP is a lot like your smartphone: it converts information from one form to another, so that it can be transmitted and received over great distances.

When you make a video of something and send it to a friend, you are actually sending digital data to them. Your smartphone detects light that is reflected off of the subject, detects sound waves, converts them to digital data, and sends them.

Your friend's smartphone receives the digital data, decodes it, lights up certain pixels that produce a representation of the original scene, and creates sound waves that are a representation of the original sound.

ESP—which is known by many names, such as *intuition, clairvoyance, psychic ability*—works in much the same way. But there are some differences.

The smartphone transmits digital data in a physical form—by way of a physical carrier.

ESP is not physical, and cannot be detected by any physical instruments. It is detected by your mind, which decodes it and transmits it to your brain, which processes the visual data in the sight centers of your brain, and processes the auditory data in the auditory region of your brain.

Since ESP is not physical—not material—we may never understand exactly *how* it works. This is so frustrating to physical scientists that they simply deny that it is even possible.

How can we prove the reality of psychic functioning? Very simple:

We can see the effects in the physical world.

The more faith you have, the better your results will be.

Even if you're not sure you believe in ESP, even if you aren't yet sure that you can use it, try it anyway. You might be surprised.

We have seen sketches from the past from painters, inventors, and other people that were left unrealized simply because they thought it was not possible in that era—or was it? Hundreds of years later it became a reality.

It did not happen in the past, maybe because they didn't trust in their imagination, trust what they built or created in their mind. Believing in it might make it a reality, but only if you follow up with it—not just make a sketch, but get busy and *do* something.

Humans were traveling to the moon in the first comic books made, and now we have been on the moon.

It might have started as science fiction, in a story book, comics, or movies, but most of all it started in the mind. The belief, expectancy, and desire become a reality only if the related action has been carried out physically and people know of it; otherwise it is not an invention.

Trust and believe in yourself.

You are an integral part of the process, and your actions matter. That is why we keep encouraging you to use your hands, and to use your imagination to imagine what something would look like or sound like or feel like.

That's why José Silva changed the meaning of *ESP*. The original term was coined by Dr. J.B. Rhine of Duke University, who called it *extrasensory perception*.

José Silva proved that ESP—psychic ability—is not an "extra" sense. It is a *prior* sense, a sense that we have always had. Everything begins with a thought. And if you wait to "perceive" something—if you just sit around and wait for something to show up—you won't get very good results. No good businessperson just sits around and waits to see if business is going show up on its own.

So Mr. Silva changed the meaning of ESP to *Effective Sensory Projection*.

You have now established points of reference in all of the material kingdoms—inanimate, plant life, and animal life—so that you can function very effectively as a psychic. We have one more thing for you to do, and that is to familiarize yourself with human anatomy, so that you can correct human health problems.

This is one of the most noble things you can do—help another human being who is suffering—and it is also the fastest way to develop your ESP.

There are many ways you can access your ESP.

Three basic forms are:

Clairvoyance: mental images

Clairaudience: mental conversations

Clairsentience: feeling what the other person is feeling.

A *clairvoyant* is one who use the brain's "clairvoyant app" to convert the subjective (psychic) information into mental pictures. You will make mental movies that reveal what is going on and will influence people to do what you want them to do. A psychic who detects information by gazing at a crystal ball is using the clairvoyant app.

A *clairaudient* will hold imaginary conversations. You will feel as though you are making up both sides of the conversation; you will imagine what you would say, and what the other person would say to you. Soon the conversation will take on a life of its own, and you will feel more like an eavesdropper than a scriptwriter. Napoleon Hill, the legendary researcher and author, wrote about having conversations with what he called "his imaginary board of directors." He was using the clairaudient app. You can do the same.

A *clairsentient* may "get a feeling" about something, or may actually feel what another person feels. You are not taking on another person's pain; you are simply becoming aware of what they are experiencing. Remember, if you ever feel uncomfortable, then use your relaxation techniques to regain full control.

A dowser who uses dowsing rods or a willow twig to locate water—or oil or precious metals—is using the clairsentient app, which produces an ideomotor response. The mind detects the information and causes a reaction in the brain, which is transmitted to the hands holding the dowsing rod or willow twig and causes a slight movement. We'll explain more below.

Oil Field Discovered with ESP

In 1920 an Oklahoma businessman named Oliver Winfield Killam discovered the biggest oil fields in the Laredo area. He knew nothing about the oil business, but at the age of 45, anticipating the financial panic of 1919, Killam had sold his business and sac-rificed his promising political career—during which he advocated and helped achieve statehood for Oklahoma—to make the jour-ney south to Laredo.

Geologists told him there was no chance of finding oil here, because the formations were too young: he had come about four million years too soon. He proved them wrong, and the land where they said there couldn't be any oil has produced more than a hundred million barrels.

A student in one of our Silva Mind Control seminars in Lar-edo told us that Killam had a set of dowsing rods mounted on the wall of his office, and used them to determine where to drill. The handles were hollow, and he put oil into them as a point of reference.

We mentioned this to José Silva, and he said that Killam actu-ally used copper tubing to make the dowsing rods. That way the crude oil filled the entire length of the dowsing rods, not just the handles.

All you need to do to make dowsing rods is bend a couple of pieces of stiff wire—like a wire coat hanger—into an L shape. Hold the short ends loosely, one rod in each hand, and point the long ends straight ahead. Keep in mind what you are looking for as you walk around. As you walk, "daydream" about what you are looking for. We explain more below about being at alpha with your eyes open when you are in a "daydreaming" state.

Dowsing rods work on the ideomotor response. So do pendu-lums, Ouija boards, and most other "paranormal" devices.

It is actually the dowser's mind that detects the presence of oil or water, or whatever he is seeking, through mental projection. Then the mind causes a reaction in the brain, which sends a tiny signal to the muscles, and as a result, the dowsing rods—which are very difficult to keep straight anyway—move. It is the ultimate form of biofeedback. It is a way to use your body to show you that your mind has detected something.

It is the person's mind that detects information through mental projection and then, through the mechanism we have mentioned, causes the pendulum to swing a certain way, or causes you to move towards a certain part of the Ouija board. During his research, José Silva conducted an experiment with one of his young subjects to see if she could detect the history of an oil well. She was able to accurately determine the age of the well, the depth, the quality of the oil, and how many barrels it produced. You can read his complete report in chapter 12.

How to Develop Your Full Potential

You can detect information using any of those methods. While everybody wants to have great, clear mental images, we don't all start off that way. Most of us actually start off by detecting information more with clairaudience and clairsentience. José Silva felt it is best if you start by sensing information and gradually develop expertise with the others.

He observed that those who start with great mental images often don't bother to develop the other means of detecting psychic information, and this limits their ability. So if you do have great mental images, remember to also use the other modes from time to time.

When programming to correct problems and do constructive and creative things, we need to use mental images. Words and feelings can help you to create mental images, but alone they are not very effective.

Remember these two things about people like Napoleon Hill and most of the others who write books about success:

1. They are among the 10 percent of humans who are natural alpha thinkers.
2. They are among the 10 percent who automatically think in mental images, or among the next 10 percent who quickly convert information that they detect into mental images.

The Science of Psychometry

One type of psychic functioning you can start using right now is called *psychometry*—the ability to detect information that has been impressed on matter. Psychometry is a good way for you to develop your intuitive ability.

In chapter 4 you projected your mind into several pieces of metal to detect information about them and familiarize yourself with them from a psychic point of view.

These metals can store information that is impressed on them. They can be altered by heat if you hold them over a candle flame. They can be magnetized. They can be altered by electricity, which is transmitted along metal wire.

The metals can also be altered by the physical part of the human aura. Your body radiates many kinds of energy. Thermometers can measure the amount of heat your body radiates. Give a bloodhound a scent, and it can track you by detecting something that your body leaves behind.

Your body radiates a collection of energies that are called the *aura*. The physical part of the aura makes impressions of everything within range, and these impressions can be detected by the human mind. The physical part of the aura extends about eight meters—25 feet—from your body.

To gain a better understanding of how psychometry works, let's listen to José Silva's explanation about how things around us work:

Everything that exists vibrates. Everything that exists has a fundamental frequency. The frequency is determined by the composition of the elements in the atoms, and the atoms in the molecules.

The total sum of atoms in a specific type of matter determines the fundamental frequency of that type of matter.

Everything is affected by light. When light comes into contact with an object, we have the fundamental frequency of the object, and we have the fundamental frequency of light. When the two collide, we end up with four frequencies:

1. The fundamental frequency of the object
2. The fundamental frequency of light
3. The sum of the two
4. The difference between the two

With our physical senses we are able to detect the difference between the two, which is *reflected*. What is reflected is what we detect with our physical senses.

The sum of the two is what is *absorbed*. We are able to detect what is absorbed with our subjective, intuitive senses.

What is reflected is affected by other reflections, by other energies.

What is absorbed is pure.

Now what do you think is the best information for you to sense:

Information with your physical senses, or

Information with your subjective senses?

The information that is absorbed is pure.

The information that is absorbed is the information that you would like to use to help you in decision making. This is what is perceived with our subjective senses.

Now we know that everything vibrates.

We sense information from the vibrations of an object.

The vibrations from your aura—the various energies that radiate from your brain and body—penetrate objects within your presence and affect the internal vibrations of objects within your aura range.

Your body radiation charges up the objects with your own frequencies.

When you touch a ring, for instance, your vibrations penetrate the ring, and it becomes an extension of you.

Anytime later, when someone touches the ring, and desires to obtain information, that person can obtain information from the vibrations in the ring.

How to Learn More about Employees and Customers

If you want to understand why an employee's performance has changed, after work sit in that employee's chair, enter your level, and imagine various scenarios in your mind until you find one that seems right to you.

If you really want to know more about what a customer or a prospect really wants and needs from a relationship with you and your business, then obtain something from the person that they have had in their possession for a while. Hold it in your left hand, enter your level, and imagine different things that might be important to them.

José Silva's brother Juan used to advise us to establish objective points of reference about new people when we meet them.

Notice what they look like, what their voice sounds like, how their hand feels when you shake hands with them. Later, when you want to program to help that person or to work on your relationship with them, you can enter your level and recall the previous impressions that you made—the points of reference. This will help you to recall more about them.

Practicing Psychometry

As you learn to function at the alpha level, you can have friends or family members bring you objects from people they know and give you a description of the people: the color of their hair, color of their eyes, complexion, maybe their height and weight.

Hold the object in the palm of your left hand and decide what information you would like to detect. Then enter your level and desire to detect that information.

Usually the information that you perceive immediately is the correct information.

Once you finish, compare your answers with the information that was provided to you.

This will help you to gain confidence and to establish points of reference showing that you are doing the right thing.

On average, an untrained person, when guessing, will be correct one out of five times.

On average, a good psychic will be correct four out of five times.

Once you have determined that you are correct more than one out of five times, you are on your way to developing better intuition.

If you wish, you can memorize this next script, record it, or have someone read it to you:

Psychometry Practice Script

Go to your center with the 3 to 1 Method. Take your time, and let me know when you are ready to proceed. (When the psychic indicates they are ready, then proceed.)

Now determine what information you are seeking. For instance, is the information that you desire physical, mental, or emotional? (pause) When you have determined this, let me know, and I will place the object in your left hand. (When the psychic indicates they are ready, then place the object in their left hand.)

Now relax and start thinking about the person who previously had this object in their possession.

Notice what impressions you get about the person's physical appearance. Is the owner of this object a male or a female? What do they look like? Perhaps you can get a feeling about their personality. Maybe you will detect information about their habitat. What kind of surroundings do they live in?

To help you detect information about the person, you can ask yourself mentally whether the person is male or female, short or tall, happy or sad. Is the person taller than my father or shorter? Notice what impressions come to you.

You may ask any kind of question you desire about this person; then clear your mind for a moment, and start thinking again to detect the answer. Tell me everything that enters your mind.

When you have a sincere desire to detect this information, because you need it to improve conditions on the planet in some manner, your mind will automatically adjust to the specific level where you will be accurate and correct.

Keep talking and tell me everything that enters your mind.

When you are done, count yourself out of level on your own.

The Green Felt Technique

Is there any such thing as a lucky charm? You can create your own "good luck" by creating your own lucky charm.

This is a technique that Juan Silva taught throughout the world in his Silva Graduate Seminars. It uses the principle of psychometry, and you can use it to help yourself and others.

First, get a small piece of green felt, the size of a piece of writing paper, or even a little smaller. After you program it, there are many ways you can use it.

You can program the piece of green felt for greater sales, improved business conditions, or any application that is necessary and beneficial for everybody concerned.

You can program it to enhance your intuitive factor, and to permeate the environment with thoughts of success.

Here is the standard procedure:

To program the green felt to help you do your job better, enter your level and objectively hold the green felt in your hands. Feel the texture. (pause) Sense it. (pause)

To program this green felt to enhance your intuitive factor, and to permeate the environment with thoughts of success, project a ray of blue-white light from the center of your forehead to the center of the green felt. (pause) This green felt will serve as a source of energy. It is a storage device. It can accumulate energy that can then be used for programming purposes. (pause)

You can program your business needs or your personal needs. Use the Three Scenes Technique to visualize the problem you wish to solve in the first scene, then in the second scene picture what you are doing to solve the problem, and then in the third scene imagine the problem solved. Project these images to the green felt. I will now allow you time to do this. (pause)

Make this piece of green felt a point of reference for what you may need in the future. (pause)

You have now programmed this piece of green felt that you have in your hands so that it will serve as a source of energy to enhance your intuitive factor, and to permeate the environment with thoughts of success.

You may hang this piece of green felt in your office, or in a high-traffic area. You may hang it in your home. You may carry it with you, so that it can serve as a source of energy anytime you need it. You may reinforce this programming whenever you desire.

Projection into the Human Kingdom

Your final mental projection exercise will be a study of human anatomy. For this, select a subject who is in good health, so that you can establish points of reference for a healthy body. You can work cases on people with health problems later on. Remember, do not select as the subject anyone who is in the room with you.

As before, you will first review your objective impressions of the person. Remember what the person looks like. Then you will explore human anatomy from a psychic point of view.

Remember that it is important to use the hands when functioning in the subjective dimension. This will help you to detect problem areas.

The best psychics we know use their hands all the time. Why, you might ask, do they need to use their hands if they are such good psychics? We would answer: one of the things that makes them great psychics is that they use their hands.

During the human anatomy conditioning cycle, we instruct you to do things that we want you to do when you are working health cases: We suggest various problems that might exist in the brain; we do the same with the heart; and also with the lungs. We want you to mentally picture what these problems would look like. This is what we mean by *projection*, and it is what we mean when we instruct you, in the Directives for Orientologists (given in the next chapter), to "allow the possibility of afflictions and malfunctions to enter your mind."

We continually remind you to use your hands, and at times even suggest that you might detect information with your hands, such as when testing for blood pressure or hardening of the arteries.

We advise you that when part of the body is removed, such as a lung or a kidney, you will still sense it as being there, but in a lighter shade or color than the rest of the body. This is the soul mold that you are detecting, the subjective "blueprint" of a perfect human body.

While these lessons are localized during the human anatomy conditioning cycle, they apply to all parts of the body. In fact, they apply to all kinds of case working, not just health cases. They also apply to relationships, business, or any other kind of case you are working.

Whenever you are projecting your mind—using remote viewing—you can use these techniques to help detect the information that you need, if this is necessary and beneficial for humanity.

Remember to correct any problems that you detect. You cannot cause a problem at a distance by thinking about the problem. This is why we don't permit you to work a case on anyone who is in the room.

However, if you detect a problem, you can correct it by attracting matter to conform to the blueprint, the soul mold, with a mental image of the malfunctioning organ now functioning in perfect health.

Time Mechanism Device

If you need to find out when a problem occurred, you can use your *time mechanism device* to do so.

To do this, use the palm of your left hand as an old-fashioned clock face. Hold your left hand up with the palm facing towards your right. Now use the forefinger of your right hand to imagine moving the hands of the clock forwards (clockwise) or backwards (counterclockwise) in time.

Each revolution will be one unit of time. You can decide what that unit of time will be: one minute, one hour, one week, one year, one decade.

For example, perhaps you are studying the person's skeleton, and you notice a line across one of their legs. You can use your time mechanism device and desire to go backwards in time 10 years with each revolution. When the line disappears, then come forward in time in small increments. You can make each revolution forward represent one year, and come forward until the line appears again. Continue moving forward and backward in time in this manner until you determine the date that the problem occurred.

As you practice this and develop your ability and confidence, you can apply it to other types of problems too. You might use it to determine how far a business or personal relationship goes back. This might help you to determine what happened so that you will be in a better position to correct the problem and improve the relationship.

It is easier to go back in time, because actions in the past have already been impressed on physics. The future, on the other hand, is composed of intentions—conceived thoughts that have not yet been materialized. Actions we intend to take have not yet been impressed on physical reality.

Human Anatomy, Part One

This is the human anatomy exercise, part one, of José Silva's UltraMind ESP System.

We will now program Effective Sensory Projection for your success. We will establish subjective points of reference in the animate-matter kingdom with reproductive intelligence and an awareness of existence. That is, we will program points of reference in the kingdom of the human body and mind, at its different levels and different depths, as we study the human anatomy from a psychic point of view.

Now we will mentally count from 10 to 1 to allow your mind to adjust to the specific level where you are going to be accurate and correct in your psychic functioning. 10 – 9 – 8 – 7 – 6 – 5 – 4 – 3 – 2 – 1. Your mind has now adjusted to the specific level where you are going to be accurate and correct in your psychic functioning.

At this time, select a relative, a friend, or a person whose face you can remember with the least effort. We will refer to this person as the *subject*. Now recall the subject's face. (pause) Now project the subject onto your mental screen. (pause) The subject is now on your mental screen. Now mentally move the subject away from the mental screen so that the screen can be used as a background. The color of the screen is black. (pause) Now mentally turn the subject's body so its left side is toward you; (pause) now turn the subject's back toward you; (pause) now turn the subject's right side toward you; (pause) now turn the subject to be facing you. (pause)

Notice how the body of the subject stands out against a black screen. (pause) The screen will now change to red. (pause) The screen is now red; notice how your subject stands out against the red screen. (pause) The screen will now change to green. (pause) The screen is now green. Notice how your subject stands out against a green screen. (pause) The screen will now change to blue. (pause) The screen is now blue; notice how your subject stands out against a blue screen. (pause) The color of the screen will now change back to green, (pause) now back to red, (pause) now back to black (pause).

Now mentally bring your subject close enough to touch. (pause) The subject is now close enough to touch. Now objectively extend your arms and place your hands, one on each side of the head. (pause) Objectively place your hands one on each side of the subject's head, your right hand over the left ear, and your left hand over the subject's right ear. (pause) Now study your subject's face and facial features: the hair, eyes, eyebrows, nose, cheeks, the character of the face. (pause) Whatever you perceive with your imagination at this dimension you can use as a point of reference in the future.

Now concentrate on your subject's forehead, and we will enter the bone-structure level within the human kingdom. (pause) Desire to detect, through visualization or imagination, bone. Bring back a memory of bone, its shape, color, and appearance. (pause) Now concentrate on the skull of your subject; study it from several angles, from the left, from the back, and from the right. (pause) Whatever you perceive with your imagination at this dimension you can use as a point of reference in the future.

Now again concentrate your attention on your subject's forehead area, and we will enter the brain-structure level. (pause) Desire to detect, through visualization or imagination, a brain. Recall your previous experience of how a brain looks; perhaps you have seen pictures of a brain. (pause) Study the brain from different angles, desiring to detect the various colors of the brain, such as gray in the front part, pink in the midpart, and dark red in the back part. (pause) Whatever you perceive with your imagination at this dimension, you can use as a point of reference in the future.

When there is brain damage, you will get an impression of black areas or spots. To help in the solution of this problem, erase the dark area or spot and form and project an impression of a healthy brain, and it is so. When you imagine a damaged area, get further impressions of the connecting nerves, which you can then follow to the possible corresponding malfunctions of the body. Damaged nerves should impress you as being oval and flat and dark in color. Healthy nerves will appear transparent and roundish. Some nerves, like those in the sensorimotor system, cross over from one side of the brain to the opposite side of the body. (pause)

Concentrate your attention on the front part of the brain again. (pause) We will now return to the bone-structure level. (pause) Get an impression of a skull. Now we will return to the outer level. (pause) We are at the outer level. Get an impression of the hair, the face, the eyes, and eyebrows.

To test the senses, you can imagine that you are superimposing the subject's head over your own, as though you were putting on a helmet. Then you will test your own senses, and whatever you feel will reflect the condition of your subject. While your subject's head is superimposed over your own, you can ask what kind of problem your subject has. You may ask whether it is psychological or physiological, and then clear your mind for a moment of time. Whatever impression comes to you immediately after this will show you the problem of your subject. You will then concentrate in this particular area. Whatever you perceive with your imagination at this dimension you can use as a point of reference in the future. Whenever you put the subject's head over your own, remember to remove it when you have completed your investigation.

Now raise the body, still facing you, and place your hands on each side of the rib cage. (pause) Begin concentrating on the center of the chest. (pause) Now we will again enter the bone-structure level within the human kingdom. (pause) You are now at the bone-structure level. Desire to detect, through visualization or imagination, the skeletal structure of your subject: the rib cage, the spinal column, the arms and legs, and the hip bones. (pause)

We are now able to detect abnormalities at this level. In the case of arthritis, for example, you will detect a powdery substance collecting on the joints of the fingers, and sometimes on the wrists, elbows, shoulder joints, and even the spinal column. The same substance will be evident in other joints where arthritis may occur, such as the toes, ankles, knees, and hip bones. (pause)

You will also be able to detect fractures, old and new. To determine when a fracture took place, use your time mechanism device. Go back in time until the perceived fracture disappears, and you will know when the fracture occurred. You can imagine that you are moving the hands of a clock. Each revolution represents whatever unit of time you desire: an hour, a day, a week, a month, a year, a decade. Whatever you perceive with your imagination at this dimension you can use as a point of reference in the future.

Now again concentrate on the center of the chest. (pause) Now we will enter the heart-tissue level within the human kingdom. (pause) We are now at the heart-tissue level. Desire to detect, through visualization or imagination, your subject's heart. (pause) Recall previous impressions and pictures of a heart, and recall how it operates. (pause) Imagine this heart, which belongs to your subject; imagine it from an external point of view; sense it; know it is there; feel it. (pause) Whatever you perceive with your imagination at this dimension you can use as a point of reference in the future.

Now the heart will become transparent. (pause) It is now transparent. Imagine how the valves function. (pause) Sometimes you will get the impression of an enlarged heart, or erratic beating, or scar tissue formations, or in some cases malfunctioning valves. (pause) Whatever you perceive with your imagination at this dimension you can use as a point of reference in the future.

To test for blood pressure, fold the fingers of your hand around an artery near the heart. Use your imagination to feel the intensity of the pulsations. (pause) If you get the impression of strong pulsations, there is high blood pressure. The strength of pulsations can also indicate normal or weak pulsations or pressure. If you get the impression that the artery gives and contracts, that it is flexible, then there is no hardening of the arteries. An impression of no flexibility means hardening of the arteries. (pause)

To test for blood chemistry, mentally draw a sample of the subject's blood and put it in an imaginary test tube. Then agitate the blood sample, and before stopping decide the purpose of the test. Once you have decided to test for the percentage of white blood cells, or sugar content, or cholesterol, or foreign chemicals, stop agitating the sample; let it settle. You will detect two different colors of blood chemistry; the less dominant color will indicate the substance you are testing for. Once you have detected what you are testing for, you will mentally ask yourself whether you are impressed with high, low, or normal content. Then clear your mind for a moment, and the first impression you receive is usually the strongest and the right one. You can repeat this operation with the same blood sample for the rest of the test. Whatever you perceive with your imagination at this dimension you can use as a point of reference in the future.

Now we will enter the lung-tissue level within the human kingdom. (pause) Desire to detect, through visualization or imagination, two lungs as they expand and contract. One lung could be a little larger than the other; this is sometimes normal. (pause) You may become aware of occasional lung problems, such as fluid at the bottom of the lungs, or of more serious conditions, such as infections, tumors, perforations, loss of elasticity, asthma, or other detectable states. Whatever you perceive with your imagination at this dimension you can use as a point of reference in the future.

Sometimes portions of a lung, or the complete lung, have to be removed through surgery. When this happens, you will detect a lighter color on the portion of lung that has been removed, or the complete lung, when removed, may be lighter. Any portion of the body that has been amputated will impress you as being lighter in color than the rest of the body. Once you have found a malfunctioning part of the body, sense it changing back to proper functioning, and let this be your final impression.

Now we will return to the heart-tissue level. (pause) Now back to the skeletal or bone-structure level; (pause) now back to the outer level. (pause) Now project the subject in front of your screen.

Your subject is now in front of your screen. Now mentally turn the subject's body so the left side is toward you; (pause) now turn the subject's back toward you; (pause) now the right side; (pause) now let the subject face you. (pause) Change the color of the screen to red. (pause) Change the color of the screen to green. (pause) Now change the color to blue. (pause)

We will change the color of the screen back to green, (pause) back to red, (pause) back to black. (pause) Now cause your subject to disappear from your screen area. (pause) Your subject has now disappeared from your screen area. Whatever you perceive with your imagination at this dimension you can use as points of reference in the future.

It is now an accomplished fact that you have established subjective points of reference in the animate matter kingdom that has reproductive intelligence and an awareness of existence, and that you now understand the established points of reference as applying to the kingdom of the human body and mind at its different levels and different depths. To function at these levels and to use these points of reference, all you need is a sincere desire to solve problems. Your mind will automatically seek out these points of reference, where you will perceive and become aware of information you can use to solve such problems. And this is so.

You have practiced entering deep, healthy levels of mind. In your next session, you will enter a deeper, healthier level of mind, faster and easier than this time.

Now when you are ready, count yourself out of your level. Take your time.

In the next exercise, you will continue with the study of human anatomy.

Human Anatomy, Part Two

When you are ready, enter your level and we will continue.

At this time, we will continue to establish subjective points of reference in the animate matter kingdom having reproductive intelligence and an awareness of existence. We will continue to investigate the kingdom of the human body and mind, at its different levels and different depths, as we establish points of reference for human anatomy from a psychic point of view.

At this time, your subject will again appear in front of your mental screen, which will now be black in color, as a background. (pause) Your subject is now in front of your mental screen. (pause) Mentally turn your subject's body so that the left side faces you; (pause) now turn the subject's back toward you; (pause) now the right side; (pause) and now have the subject face you. (pause)

Notice how the body of the subject will stand out against the color of the screen when the color of the screen changes. The screen will now change to red. (pause) The screen will now change to green. (pause) The screen will now change to blue. (pause) The color of the screen will now turn back to green, (pause) now back to red, (pause) now back to black. (pause)

Now you will bring your subject close enough to touch. (pause) The subject is now close enough to touch. Now you will objectively extend your arms and place your hands one on each side of the rib cage. (pause) Place your hands on each side of the subject's rib cage: place your left hand on the subject's right side and your right hand on the subject's left side. (pause)

Now concentrate on the center of the chest. (pause) Now we will again enter the bone-structure level of the human kingdom. (pause) You are now at the bone-structure level. Desire to detect, through visualization or imagination, the skeletal body of your subject; begin by concentrating on the rib cage. (pause) Now we will enter the stomach-tissue level within the human kingdom. (pause) Desire to detect, through visualization or imagination, your subject's stomach; recall your previous experience for an accurate impression of a stomach. (pause) Whatever you perceive with your imagination at this dimension, you can use as a point of reference in the future.

Some of the more common problems of the stomach area are ulcers, tumors, obstructions, and the improper balance of gastric juices. In the case of surgery, when a portion of the stomach has been removed, you will get the impression of an entire stomach, with the missing part sensed in a lighter shade or color that contrasts with the rest of the stomach.

Now we will enter the level to sense the intestinal tract. (pause) Desire to detect, through visualization or imagination, the intestinal tract as it begins at the outlet of the stomach. The first part of the small intestine is called the *duodenum*. (pause) Some of the problems of the intestines are much the same as those of the stomach, and many of these same problems carry over to the large intestine at the lower right side of the trunk of the body, where the appendix is located. (pause) The colon, or large intestine, goes up on the right side of the body to a level just below the liver, then crosses below the stomach to the left side of the body. The part of the colon that goes up on the right side of the body is called the *ascending colon*; the part of the colon that crosses over from the right to left is called the *transverse colon*; the remaining part, which comes down on the left side of the body, is called the *descending colon.* (pause) Whatever you perceive with your imagination at this dimension you can use as a point of reference in the future.

Now we will concentrate on the pancreas at that particular tissue level. (pause) Desire to detect, through visualization or imagination, the pancreas: it is slightly below and behind the stomach. It is an elongated gland that feeds its digestive juices through a duct in the duodenum. (pause) An obstructed duct could prevent the enzymes from entering the duodenum. The pancreas contains islands of cells that produce a hormone called *insulin*, which is released directly into the bloodstream. An impression of black spots, or islands, on the pancreas could indicate diabetes. Light spots, or islands, on the pancreas could indicate hypoglycemia. (pause) Whatever you perceive with your imagination at this dimension you can use as a point of reference in the future. A final impression of a properly functioning and healthy pancreas is recommended for better health.

Now we will enter the liver-tissue level within the human kingdom. (pause) Desire to detect, through visualization or imagination, the liver. The liver is a little higher than the pancreas, and to the right in the person's body. (pause) It has been said by psychics that if the liver gives a shiny impression, it is healthy. If it is dull, a problem exists. There could be one of several things wrong. There could be an enlargement of the liver, tumors, or infections. (pause) Whatever you perceive with your imagination at this dimension you can use as a point of reference in the future.

Now we will enter the gall bladder level within the human kingdom. (pause) Desire to detect, through visualization or imagination, the gall bladder. (pause) The gall bladder is attached to the liver. It has a duct that joins the pancreatic duct to form the common duct into the duodenum. (pause) Stone formations could exist in the duct of any gland. When you perceive an impression of stone formations in the gall bladder or in any duct, imagine going through the process of crushing the stones into a fine powder with your fingers, and imagine the powder dissolving in the gland's secretions. Your last impression of the gall bladder should be a healthy one, with no stone formations. (pause) Whatever you perceive with your imagination at this dimension you can use as a point of reference in the future.

Now we will enter the kidney-tissue level within the human kingdom. (pause) Desire to detect, through visualization or imagination, two kidneys. You have seen pictures of kidneys before; get an impression of them as being solid, from an outer point of view. (pause) Sometimes one kidney is a larger than the other, and sometimes one is a little higher, but this could be a normal condition. (pause) Whatever you perceive with your imagination at this dimension you can use as a point of reference in the future.

Now we will perceive the kidneys as transparent. (pause) Desire to sense the kidneys as transparent. If you detect these filtering systems as processing unequally or differently from each other, then something could be wrong, such as an infection. An infection could travel up from the bladder to the kidney, or from the kidney to the bladder. Stone formations also could hinder the functioning of a kidney. When this is the case, imagine crushing the stone formations into fine powder with your fingers, and imagine the powder dissolving in the urine. Whatever you perceive with your imagination at this dimension you can use as a point of reference in the future.

When you get an impression that both kidneys are not quite functioning well, but you are not sure why, then compare the subject's kidneys to those of a healthy person who has no kidney problems. The final impression should always be one of health. (pause)

We will go back to the gall bladder level, (pause) to the liver level, (pause) to the pancreas level, (pause) to the intestinal tract level, (pause) to the stomach level, (pause) to the skeletal body level, (pause) now back to the outer level. (pause)

We are now at the outer level of the human kingdom. Here you can study the outer skin by desiring to perceive it through visualization or imagination. (pause) You can detect skin problems, such as infections, allergies, tumors, injuries, or scars. Whatever you perceive with your imagination at this dimension you can use as a point of reference in the future.

Now project your subject back in front of the screen. (pause) Mentally turn the subject's body so the subject's left side faces you. (pause) Now turn the subject's back toward you. (pause) Now the right side. (pause) Now allow the subject to face you. (pause)

Change the color of the screen to red. (pause) Change the color of the screen to green. (pause) Now change the color to blue. (pause)

The color of the screen will now change back to green, (pause) back to red, (pause), back to black. (pause) Now imagine your subject in perfect health. (pause) Now cause your subject to disappear from the screen. (pause) Your subject has now disappeared from the screen area.

Whatever you perceive with your imagination at this dimension you can use as points of reference in the future.

It is now an accomplished fact that you have established subjective points of reference in the animate matter kingdom having reproductive intelligence and an awareness of existence, and you understand how these points of reference apply to the kingdom of the human body and mind at its different levels and different depths. To function at these levels and to use these points of reference, all you need is a sincere desire to solve problems. Your mind will automatically seek out these points of reference, where you will perceive and become aware of information you can use to solve problems. And this is so.

You have practiced entering deep, healthy levels of mind. In your next session, you will enter a deeper, healthier level of mind, faster and easier than this time.

Now when you are ready, count yourself out of your level. Take your time.

Tips on How to Proceed

Remember: if you record these instructions and listen to the recording, or if you have someone read them to you, then you can do the entire exercise—both segments—in one session.

If you are memorizing what to do and then doing it on your own without anybody guiding you, then it will be easier to do it one segment at a time.

The next chapter contains detailed information about working health cases in order to help people who are sick and hurting, and to improve your ESP.

Also remember to continue to practice the Silva Centering Exercise. We recommend practicing it between each of these mental projection exercises, the same as we do in the live seminars:

✗ Silva Centering Exercise

✗ Projection to Home

✗ Silva Centering Exercise

✗ Projection into Inanimate Matter Kingdom

✗ Silva Centering Exercise

✗ Projection into Plant Life Kingdom

✗ Silva Centering Exercise

✗ Projection into Animate Matter Kingdom

✗ Silva Centering Exercise

✗ Projection into Human Kingdom

After you have completed the training, then you can maintain your ability by using what you have learned to solve problems. We recommend that you go to the alpha level at least once a day, for five minutes. Twice a day is better, three times a day is excellent.

To practice for five minutes each time is good, 10 minutes is better, 15 minutes is excellent.

How to Test Your Intuition

To complete your degree in business intuition, there is one more step to take:

Put what you have learned to use by working at least 10 health cases. Use your ESP to detect health problems in 10 different people, and mentally correct all of the abnormalities that you become aware of.

You can develop your intuition by working health detection and correction cases.

In order to learn to "read minds," you first begin by learning to "read bodies."

José Silva recommends that you evaluate your progress over a sample of 10 health detection and correction cases.

The idea is to detect the information mentally, and then verify objectively that you were accurate.

What do we mean by health cases?

Working a health case is very similar to what you did in the human anatomy conditioning cycle. At your level, you scan the body of a person who is sick or injured, with a desire to become aware of what their problem is.

Then, after you make a thorough investigation and identify everything that you suspect could be a problem, you get feedback and find out about all of the known problems.

You compare the known problems with what you identified during your investigation, and use this information to help you improve your ability to accurately detect problems.

Not everything that you detect will be a problem. This is a good thing: if you don't have any "misses," then you will not be able to learn how to recognize your "hits."

After you have reviewed your experience in this matter, you will correct every problem that you are aware of—every problem that you detected, even those that were not confirmed, and any problems you didn't detect but were told about.

To correct a problem, you create a mental picture of the problem part of the body in perfect health. This mental image will help to attract matter back to conform to the soul mold of a perfect human body.

In seminars, we have an *orientologist* to present cases to each student, who is referred to as a *psychic*. Below are the Directives for Orientologists. You can read through them to see exactly how the process works. When you are ready, you can record these directions and guide yourself to work health cases, or have someone read them to you, or do it on your own.

After you read through the Directives for Orientologists, we will discusses health case working some more, and will answer the questions that students typically have.

Directives for Orientologists

(Health problems

Presenting problem cases to beginners for psychic investigation.)

1. a. Enter your laboratory level by the 3 to 1, 10 to 1 Method.

   b. If you have worked cases before, review a case about which you were accurate before working a new one.

   c. Let me know when you are ready. (When ready, continue.)

   d. I will now count from 10 to 1 to allow your mind to adjust to the specific level where you are going to be accurate and correct on the problem case that I am going to present to you. $10 - 9 - 8 - 7 - 6 - 5 - 4 - 3 - 2 - 1$. Your mind has now adjusted to the specific level where you are going to be accurate and correct about the case I am going to present to you.

2. a. At the count of three, the image of the body of (give name, age, address, and sex of subject) will be on your screen.

   b. $1 - 2 - 3$. (snap fingers) The image of the body of (give name, age, address, and sex of subject) is on your screen.

   c. Sense it, (pause) feel it, (pause) visualize it, (pause) know it is there, (pause) take it for granted it is there.

   d. Now that you have the subject in front of you, let us analyze what kind of problem we are going to deal with. It could be health, family relations, or business. Allow the different possibilities to enter your mind, and determine which is strongest and is the one that you want to work on: health, family relations, or business.

(Orientologist: If the problem is family relations or business, let the psychic report whatever he or she is inclined to say about the problem situation. When finished, or if they select a health problem, continue with 3.)

3. a. Slowly scan the body with your sensing faculties, starting at the scalp and moving your sensing faculties downwards inch by inch until you reach the feet. Let me know when you move your sensing faculties from one point to the other. You must keep talking as you go.

   b. As you continue to scan the body with your sensing faculties, continue to talk as you go, and tell me everything that enters your mind about the subject. Whenever you feel that there is a problem, let me know.

(Orientologist: When you notice the psychic getting near the problem area, mentally project a thought or mental picture of the problem. This helps the psychic to develop a feeling for clairvoyance.)

   c. This is a practice session; at this time, let your experience come forth. Accuracy comes with practice.

   d. You may feel as though you are guessing, so tell me everything that enters your mind.

(Orientologist: as soon as the psychic detects a problem, have them zoom in on it.)

e. Amplify the select area or part of the body, zoom in on it, analyze it, and tell me what you detect with your sensing faculties.

f. When you locate the area of the body that is doubtful, think of the possible problems that could affect this part of the body. Remember, once you detect a problem, apply the corrective measures that you feel are appropriate.

(Orientologist: when the psychic has finished with that part of the body, instruct them to continue scanning the rest of the body.)

g. After you have corrected what you detected, continue scanning the body, moving your sensing faculties downwards inch by inch until you reach the feet.

h. Keep talking as you investigate; tell me everything that you are inclined to say. You may feel as though you are making it up; this is the correct feeling. Tell me your impressions regardless of whether you think they are right or wrong.

(Orientologist: Be sure to have information written down ahead of time. When you notice the psychic getting near the problem area, mentally project a thought or a mental picture of the problem to the psychic. This helps the psychic to develop a feeling for clairvoyance.

In the beginning, encourage "hits" by telling the psychic to tell all. Do not say "right" or "wrong" until a complete report has been given.

After a complete report has been given by the psychic, then at that time evaluate the information, tell the psychic what you know about the case, and point out the hits to the psychic so that they can be reviewed by the psychic while at level. During this evaluation, with misses, tell the psychic, "I do not have this information; it could be so."

On hits, remind the psychic to review the information perceived with the subjective senses, and especially the feeling experienced when the psychic said what he or she said, in order to establish points of reference while still at level.

If everything is a total miss, the psychic could have the wrong person. The best thing to do is to present a new case.

Be sure to have psychic send correction for the problems detected, at the completion of a case and before working another case or coming out of level.

After this is done, you can give the psychic another case by going back to paragraph 2a.

The following is to be said aloud to the psychic when the psychic has completed the case working session and is ready to come out of level.)

4. a. Every time you enter this dimension with the sincere
       desire to help humanity, you will be helping yourself.
       Your talents will increase, and you will become more
       accurate every time. And this is so.
    b. Thank you. You may thank your counselors, say the
       farewell prayer, and come out, 1 to 10, 1 to 3,
       in perfect health.

Discuss the case briefly.

Special Instructions

1. We do not diagnose. Only medical people have license to diagnose and heal. We conduct psychic investigation for detection and correction of abnormalities at a psychic level and at a distance.

2. We do not perform psychic investigation of a person when that person is present.

3. We do not give our own name to be worked as a case while we are present.

4. We avoid involvement that blocks our ability to function.

5. We do not create problems. We solve problems.

6. Avoid talking about negative things when a person is at deep levels.

7. Work with human life before working on animal life, plant life, and the inanimate. Never neglect human life.

How to Perfect Your Problem-Solving Ability

You have within you everything that you need to correct any problem you detect and to cope with any situation you encounter, provided you are willing to work at it and use the tools and talents you possess.

Case working serves as an ideal example of how to deal with problems, and provides a perfect form of practice for perfecting your subjective skills.

Information is always available to you when you have a need for it. You must be able to recognize it and convert it to a form that you can use to help you correct problems.

Working health cases offers you an ideal way to learn to sense information accurately through the use of your imagination, and then to practice subjectively correcting problems with the use of your imagination.

Working health cases will help you develop the skills you need to correct every other kind of problem: finances, business, relationships, self-image, personal growth, decision making, stress management, and anything else you can think of.

To correct problems, you need first to be aware that a problem exists. If you don't know that a problem exists, you won't know that it needs to be corrected. Then you need to know exactly what the problem is. You need to know the correct technique to apply, and how to apply the technique correctly.

Working health cases is the easiest way to perfect your problem-solving ability.

When you confirm objectively that you have accurately determined the problem mentally, then you know that you are at the correct level to obtain information subjectively.

At first, as you learn to use your visualization and imagination faculty to detect information, you will become aware of many impressions. Some of these impressions will be information that is accurate; other impressions may come from your own creative abilities.

As you practice working cases, you will learn to tell the difference. You will become more and more accurate at telling when you have the correct information as you continue to practice.

How do you learn? Through objective feedback. As you work your cases, you will be able to verify that you have detected problems accurately, and establish points of reference that you can use to help you be more accurate in the future.

The information is there for you. It comes as an emotional or mental feeling, like a sense of knowing. As you get these feelings, you express them as mental pictures or words or physical feelings. That is why the orientologist tells the psychic first to sense or visualize an image of a body. When you begin to work a case, you can simply visualize (recall) the body of somebody you know who is the same age and sex as the case.

Next, you scan the body in detail, looking for problems. Do not wait for something to come to you. You could treat it like a true-false test: if you want to know whether there is a problem with the subject's brain, then allow the possibility of afflictions and malfunctions to enter your mind. Imagine a damaged brain compared to a healthy brain. Do you get a feeling that one image or the other is the correct one?

Remember that José Silva calls this *Effective Sensory Projection.* We do not sit by, passively waiting for something to happen. Instead, project your sensing faculties and look for problems that need to be corrected. Think of the problem. Mentally picture the problem, and you will be able to tell if this is the correct picture or not. You do not want to do this if you are in the person's presence, but you cannot cause harm by doing it at a distance.

Gain as Much Experience as Possible

When you are working health-detection cases, tell the orientologist everything you detect. At this point, your job is to get as much experience as you can, so say everything that you feel like saying.

Your orientologist will provide feedback for all known problems. That way you can review and note the difference in the feeling you had when you were correct, compared to when you might have been making it up.

After you have practiced the "Magic 50" health cases and correctly detected dozens of problems, you will begin to be much more confident and much more accurate, because you will be better able to determine when you are detecting accurate information.

Then, when you are working on other kinds of problems, you will know exactly when you are at the ideal level to do your subjective work. You will know exactly when you are detecting and receiving accurate information rather than making it up.

How to Become More Accurate

When you enter your level, review your most recent, most successful case. This will help you get back to the same level again, and be just as accurate on your next case.

Always remember to work on real problems, not hypothetical, make-believe ones. The mind is designed to correct real problems, not to play games. People who play games lose their accuracy, while those who put their abilities to work on authentic problems that need to be corrected increase their ability to correct problems and achieve their goals.

Continue to practice working health cases on a regular basis, and you will continue to maintain and increase your abilities. Form the habit of working a case on each member of your family every night. Whenever you detect a possible problem, correct it.

Case working is one of the most unselfish acts you can perform, and also one of the best things you can do to help yourself.

Be advised, however, that José Silva always cautioned that you should be working health cases because people need help and you have the ability to help them. If you are only working them for the benefits that you will receive, you will not gain all of the benefits that you could be gaining.

The key to success is practice, practice, practice.

It is usually easy to work three or four cases before coming out of level.

After you have worked 10 cases in this manner, evaluate your accuracy for the test sample of 10 health cases that you worked.

Answers to Questions about Working Health Cases

What do you do to correct the problems? Use anything that will help you to correct the problem. Use the Three Scenes Technique to move from problem to solution. Create tools and medicines with your mind if they will help you imagine correcting the problem. They can be old-fashioned, modern, or futuristic. Use anything that produces results. The bottom line is: did it correct a problem? If it corrected or prevented a problem and improved conditions, that's what you want to use until you find something better.

How many times should I work a case? If you can obtain information about the person's progress, then you can continue working the case until the person is healthy. If you are working a case on someone you don't know and you are not able to get new information about their health, working the case once is enough. However, trust your intuition: if you think about the case, that might mean that your intuition is telling you to enter your level and reinforce the corrections that you made.

How often should I work the case? Work the case and apply the correction whenever you think you should. Watch for feedback, and let your results guide you. When there is some improvement, keep doing what you have been doing. If the person gets worse, do something different.

Is there some place where I can get health cases to work? Yes, there is a website that was set up by an appreciative Silva graduate where people who need help post their health problems so that Silva graduates worldwide can work their cases and help them. The address is in Appendix D.

Can you work a health case on yourself? Yes, you can. Just project an image of your body onto your mental screen, just as you would with someone else's body.

How Feedback Guides You

A young man (27 years old at the time) who was getting ready for a kidney transplant came to class in Laredo. Our graduate support group really worked hard on him in our weekly meetings.

He said it saved his life, literally.

When he finally got the transplant, he never needed painkillers for pain, and made a great recovery.

We saw him a couple of years later during instructor training. He told us he was married, everything was great, and he owned it all to the class that we had insisted he attend.

One problem for Jerry was a high number on one of his ongoing lab tests, and the doctors were concerned about it. It was supposed to be below 2, and his was sometimes over 30! Every time we programmed to lower the number, it got higher! We don't know why, but that happens sometimes.

After the surgery, it was down to 2.5, and they were trying to lower it. We programmed, and the next day it was 2.7. We kept programming, and it went up to 2.9.

Then an idea came to us. We asked Jerry if they could settle for the count being at 2.5, considering how high it had been before. He said yes; there were some people with counts over 3, and they were OK.

So we stopped worrying about it, and stopped programming for it. Guess what: it went down!

Why? Who knows! What matters is: do whatever works. If it gets better when you stop programming, then stop programming! That's not how we expect it to work, but who cares! Just do whatever works.

When you feel that the person needs more programming, then program, and notice what happens. That's how to know how often to program. Trust your intuition, and let the results tell you if you are doing the right thing.

During his research, Mr. Silva wanted to know if he was really on to something or not. So he selected 10 people in Laredo who had health problems from which they were not expected to recover. He started programming for them, as we have described. He did what he felt needed to be done.

His idea was that if one of those people recovered, that by itself didn't mean much; it might have happened anyway. But if two got well, that had scientific validity. It would mean he was on to something.

Over the course of the next three years, as he continued to program for those people, every one of them recovered. Everyone got well. What a powerful message!

You Are Multidimensional and Multitasking

If there were a way that you could learn to function as a psychic with your eyes open, would you like to know about it?

With some practice, you can learn to do exactly that.

Little by little, as you get used to it, you don't have to use all of the procedures that you had to use in the beginning, when you were first learning how to function at level.

Here's the secret: your brain dips into alpha frequently. In fact, your brain takes little trips to alpha approximately 30 times every minute. For an untrained and inexperienced person, the brain only remains at level for a few microseconds. If the person has not established points of reference in the subjective dimension and practiced functioning there with conscious awareness, they will not even realize that this is happening.

But for a graduate of the UltraMind ESP System who has practiced working health cases, these dips into alpha can be used.

Clairvoyance with Open Eyes

It doesn't take a lot of practice to learn to function with eyes open anytime you need to.

In fact, the formula is included in the human anatomy conditioning cycle in chapter 7.

When you have worked 10 health cases, as you are supposed to do before graduating, you no longer need to use the complete 3 to 1, 10 to 1 deepening ritual to enter your clairvoyant level. You can shorten it to just 10 to 1.

When you have worked another 10 cases and continue to be satisfied with your results, you can use the 3 to 1 Method alone for entering your level.

When you have worked still another 10 cases and you continue to be satisfied with the results, then all you need to do is to close your eyes and take one deep breath, and while exhaling, you will enter your clairvoyant level.

Once you are completely satisfied with your results, you can function with your eyes open when needed. Your desire to function at your clairvoyant level with your eyes open will cause the so-called daydream mechanism to function at your clairvoyant level. From then on your daydreaming will take place at your clairvoyant level, and to enter it, just daydream. At that time controlled daydreaming will be "creative" and the "true reality."

To reach that point, test yourself on a sample size of 10 cases. That's enough to give you an accurate idea of how well you are doing. If you are satisfied with your accuracy over that sample, then move to the next step. If not, then work 10 more cases using the same procedure for entering your level as before. Once you are satisfied, move on to the next level.

It takes as few as 50 cases to complete this entire procedure. That's a very small investment to learn how to function as a psychic with your eyes open whenever you need to.

Eventually, as you continue to practice and to correct problems whenever you become aware of them, this will become a natural event. You will not even have to think about going to your level. You will simply become aware of information that you can use to correct problems.

Correcting a Back Problem

You don't need mental images in order to *detect* problems. The majority of people don't have good mental images. I don't. I usually detect information with my hands—as if I were actually feeling it with my hands.

We do need mental images to *correct* problems. We have already mentioned the soul mold, which is like a blueprint of a perfect body for each of us. Matter conforms to that mold. When matter gets out of that mold, the soul mold tries to attract it back, like a magnet under a piece of paper attracting iron filings. Our mental image will reinforce the soul mold, and will help it to attract matter back to the shape of a perfect human body.

It doesn't matter how you do it, as long as you finish with an image of perfect health.

Whatever information you transmit will end up helping. It cannot hurt, and if your intention is to help, it will help. Your mind and the receiver's mind will make sure of that, just the way smartphones handle data correctly.

If you don't see any progress within three days, try something different. Do whatever comes to mind. If it is a serious problem, use any and every technique you think might help. Let your results guide you: If the person gets better, do more of what you are doing. If they get worse, do the opposite. If nothing happens, do something else.

During his research, Mr. Silva used to invite the public, and he would have his young research subjects work cases on those with health problems. One man had back pain, so the child who worked the case said that one of the vertebrae in his lower back was out of line. She pushed it back into line. He felt better. The pain was gone for a couple of days.

When he came back the next week, he said the pain had returned. She worked the case again, and said she realized what had happened: the vertebra had "rebounded" and gone back out of line—like a swing swinging back and forth. So this time she pushed it beyond the center point, so that when it rebounded and came back, it would stop in perfect alignment. Evidently it did, because he didn't have any more pain after that.

Do whatever it takes to correct the problem.

The Magic 50 Health Cases

Now that you have worked your first 10 health cases with satisfactory results, you have earned the equivalent of a bachelor's degree in business intuition.

To earn your MBI—your master's degree in business intuition—work what Sam Gonzalez Silva has dubbed the Magic 50 health cases.

When you have done this, you will find that your ability to detect information with your mind is becoming just as natural as detecting information with your eyes and ears and smell and taste and touch.

You don't have to think about what to do with your eyes when you want to know what something looks like: you just look at it. When somebody talks to you, you don't need to stop and think about how to use your sense or hearing; you just listen to them.

Your mind is the master sense of human intelligence, and you can learn to use it to detect information just as easily and naturally as you use your other senses.

One thing we teach—you may recall it from the last conditioning cycle—is to evaluate your proficiency over test samples of

10 health cases. If you are satisfied with your results, then shorten the ritual, until eventually you can work cases—project your mind and detect information—even with your eyes open, but not focused on anything specific in the environment. It may feel like you are daydreaming.

How long does it take to develop the ability to use this day-dreaming state to detect information accurately?

As little as 50 health cases. After each 10 cases, evaluate your accuracy. If you are satisfied with your results, then shorten the ritual. With as little as five sets of 10 cases each, you will be able to use your intuition even with your eyes open whenever you need to use it to solve a problem.

Psi-Missing

J.B. Rhine, a pioneer in the science of parapsychology, was the first to note the phenomenon of psi-missing—a score of incorrect results so consistent that it is as significant as a high proportion of hits. It even begins to look like a deliberate attempt to miss the target.

In the everyday world we call psi-missers "born losers."

One executive told the author how his company uses its resident born loser. He was the company treasurer—excellent with figures and with decision making where data was valid and available. However, when a decision had to be made that called for intuition, the company gave the problem to the treasurer, got his intuitive decision, and then proceeded to do the opposite. The executive relating the story claimed a very high level of success using this method.

How "Failure" Can Help You Win

A very successful athletic coach said recently that if you never lose, you won't learn what it takes to win.

A retired championship crew chief was providing commentary during practice for a NASCAR stock car race one day. He observed that one of the young drivers was getting closer and closer to hitting the wall on every lap. "He wants to see how close he can get to it," the old crew chief said.

The very next lap, the driver hit the wall. "Now he knows," the crew chief said. "Not that close."

Hector Chacon, a local high school basketball coach, attended class with us in Laredo. He had been a member of the last state championship team from Laredo. He had been successful coaching at a local high school in the past, but was in a slump.

When it came time for case working, he missed every case. We watched, and thought we saw something, so we took over and presented three cases to him and confirmed what we thought we had seen. The third case was a Catholic nun we knew personally who had been in a serious auto accident and had sustained a severe head injury that left her disabled. Recently she had developed cataracts, and her vision was quite bad.

Coach Chacon scanned her body and went right to her feet. That's all he could come up with. After he came out of level, we pointed out to him that he was selecting areas as far from where the problem was as possible.

If there was a problem in the head, he went to the feet. If it was on the front of the body, he went to the back; if on the left side, he chose the right.

It was very late, and we had one more session two nights later, so we told him that during the next two days, he should go to his level and analyze what he had done. When he came back to the final session and worked more cases, he should do the opposite of whatever he was doing the previous night.

When he came back for the final session, he was 100 percent accurate on every case he worked. Being a championship athlete and coach, he was very confident that he could do whatever we told him to do, so he didn't seem nearly as impressed as we were with his case working accuracy that night.

We asked him what he did differently.

He said, "I just did what you told me to."

"How did you do it? What was it exactly that you did?"

"I just followed your instructions," he said.

At that point, we recalled the old saying, "If it works, don't fix it," and we didn't pursue it any further. So we cannot tell you how he did it, and that is probably appropriate. We each need to learn for ourselves the difference between what works and what doesn't work.

Coach Chacon applied what he had learned when coaching his basketball team the following season. They weren't the most talented players he'd ever had, and they weren't the tallest, and the local experts had predicted that they would have a losing season and finish near the bottom in the district.

Instead, they won almost every game and won the bi-district championship. He said they didn't make any changes to the way they played basketball. They still dribbled and passed and shot the same way. The change was how they used their minds.

You'll never learn how far you can go—how close you can come to failure—until you go just a little bit too far, just as the young race driver did. By the way, he went on to win two championships.

While we can learn from our "failures" that way, we don't want to dwell on them. After it has served its purpose, just recall your successes.

Leveraging Your Successes

José Silva said that we used to tell people to learn from their failures. Now we tell you to learn from your successes.

There is a special feeling that comes with success, and the only way to get that feeling, Mr. Silva said, is to have a success.

You can also go to your level and recall your successes. Every time you enter your level and recall a success—and recall that special feeling of success—it is almost as valuable as having a new success. The more successes you have, the more confidence you will have, and the easier it will be to have more, and bigger, successes in the future.

This applies to every aspect of your life. When you make a great presentation and your ideas are adopted, then, as soon as you have an opportunity, enter your level and review everything you did, especially the special feeling of success, in order to reinforce it.

The Best Time to Begin

Careful research has revealed that the best time to begin this program, which will enable you to function at your level by simply daydreaming, is—right now.

Today is the only time you can do anything. If you wait until tomorrow, then tomorrow becomes today, so you still have to begin today.

It's like the sign in the bar in Arizona that reads, "Free beer tomorrow." If you go there tomorrow, guess what the sign will say? That's right: "Free beer tomorrow."

You have within you everything you need to correct any problem you detect and to cope with any situation you encounter, provided you are willing to work at it and use the tools and talents you possess.

Working health cases offers you an ideal way to learn to sense information accurately through the use of your visualization, and then to practice subjectively correcting problems with the use of your imagination.

Information is always available to you when you have a need for it. You must be able to recognize it, even when it come in subjective (psychic) form, and convert it to a form that you can use to help you correct problems.

Part Two

How to Use Your Mind
to Increase Productivity

Subjective Persuasion

Most of your success in business probably depends on how well you deal with people.

Have you ever stopped to think about how many different people you interact with—customers, suppliers, employees, superiors, subordinates, salespeople, creative people, regulators, shareholders, con artists, crooks?

Sometimes you interact with people individually, other times in a group. Sometimes you interact face-to-face, other times at a distance. Sometimes you interact with people you never meet through your advertising and marketing efforts.

Our Responsibility as Humans

Plants can be programmed, but they cannot program. Inanimate matter can be programmed, but cannot program. Only humans can program.

That puts you in control here on planet earth. You are in control of your circumstances, in control of your good fortune, in control of your life. With guidance from higher intelligence, you can solve problems and improve living conditions on the planet, so that when we move on, we will have left behind a better world for those who follow.

In this chapter, we will show you ESP techniques that you can use in your various interactions, including techniques you can use in advance, in person, and afterwards.

While your objective interactions may take place at a specific time, your subjective (mental) interactions can take place anytime, anyplace, with anybody, even if you don't know exactly whom you are interacting with.

You can use this subjective interaction to get your point across to the other person, or to let them get their point across to you so that you know better how to serve their needs and help them achieve their objectives. This is one of the best ways to comply with the Laws of Programming and make sure that the best thing is done for everyone concerned.

When all of the brain is working, instinct and intuition come through. The more people who are working together in harmony, the more you can accomplish.

A Multipurpose Programming Technique

You can use the Three Scenes Technique, which you learned in chapter 5, to communicate one-on-one, to get a message to a group, to provide damage control after a problem has occurred, to prevent misunderstandings and future problems, to encourage a change in attitude and behavior, to reassure, and to do whatever else you need to do.

As with case working, there are many ways you can detect information from your subject. You can imagine asking questions and imagine how your subject would answer. Sometimes new ideas and insights emerge that you have never thought of before.

When you need to persuade your subject to do what you believe is best for everyone concerned, mental images work best. You can use words to help you create good mental images.

How to Have Greater Subjective Influence

Whenever you are talking to someone, remember to project mental pictures to them.

When you are telling them the benefits they can expect from doing what you are asking them to do, mentally picture them enjoying those benefits.

When you ask someone to do a task, mentally picture them doing exactly what it is that you want them to do.

You might have done that when you were young. Did you ever stare at somebody and imagine them turning to look at you until they did? Or perhaps you were the one who was stared at. Imagine how this concept can be applied for correcting subordinates, reassuring superiors, persuading customers, convincing suppliers to accept your offer, and more.

As we mentioned in chapter 8, you are multidimensional and multitasking. In addition to using your physical eyes to see what things look like, you can project your mind into the very heart of things and detect information that you cannot detect with your physical senses.

At first you learn to do one or the other. Soon you will be doing both without giving it a second thought. Just as you look at somebody and listen to them at the same time, you can add another sense: your mind.

An ER Doctor Serves Patients Better

A doctor can use these techniques to help diagnose a patient quickly. Doctors observe many things about patients—what their skin looks like, their eyes, their body language, their facial expression. A Silva-trained doctor can also project within to the soul mold. The doctor's mind will quickly detect any matter that does not conform to the blueprint.

The doctor might detect that blood is not flowing freely from the heart, and will order an ultrasound to confirm it. No further tests will be needed; treatment can start immediately.

Dr. Calvin Poole of Gloster, Mississippi, does that regularly, and as a result he makes much more efficient use of his time while reducing costs to his patients and getting faster results. Here are some experiences he sent us recently:

> While working the ER, I was seeing a lot of patients with stomach viruses. It is not always the excitement that one sees on television. With so many people coming in, it is impossible and unnecessary to do a full workup on everyone.
>
> I picked up one of the charts and a voice said, "This one has an appendicitis." I told the nurses, and they said, "But you

haven't even seen the patient yet." I went ahead and started a workup on him. Everything was equivocal, so I did a CT (computerized tomography) with IV (intravenous) and oral contrast. This showed up an appendicitis!

What was weird is that another patient came in several days later, and it was a replay of the same thing. Pick up the chart, make the diagnosis, get the studies ordered, see the patient—not the usual pattern for diagnosis. The surgeon called me later and told me that he had an early appendicitis, but not bad.

I have had some emergencies come in, and wondered, "How in the world am I going to manage this?" I got out of the way and let something else take over, and got good results on all of them.

I had one episode of a woman stepping on a nail, and it breaking off in her foot. Removing it is one of the most difficult things to do, with all the tendons and connective tissue. It was a very small nail, like an upholstery nail, not much bigger than a straight pin.

Suddenly the idea of using fluoroscopy came up. I think someone said it, but who knows?

I went back and worked on it for about 45 minutes. I could get close, but could not get it. I said, "I give up," clicked the hemostats closed, which I normally would not have done, pulled them out, and they had the nail that I had been looking for.

Thanks again on behalf of both me and my patients, most of whom would not have believed the method that I was trained in and used.

Persuading Dishonest People to Be Honest

A lady in Bulgaria who took the UltraMind ESP System seminar with Milen Mihaylov used the UltraMind techniques to prevent unscrupulous people from defrauding her. Here is her story.

A year and a half ago I attended a workshop for the Silva Ultra-Mind ESP System with instructor Milen Mihaylov. Inspired by what I had learned about the system, I immediately began to apply it in regards to an issue of mine that had become quite pressing in recent years. Looking back, this is what happened and what change I was able to bring.

My parents wanted to buy an apartment in the town where I lived. I started looking for offers, visiting real estate for sale and comparing prices. So I came to meet a lawyer who was then working with a company that was building and selling properties. He showed me a few apartments that I liked and that were at a good price.

I called my parents to come to visit the apartments. They liked one, so we asked the lawyer to prepare a preliminary agreement for the purchase. The contract was drawn up, and immediately afterwards we paid by bank transfer half of the selling price as an advance payment for the finalization of the deal. The deal itself was to take place no later than three months after. This period was necessary since the apartment was to be purchased through the lawyer, who was preparing everything, and not directly from the developer.

Three months passed, then six months, and still no deal. Something would come up every time to prevent the deal—

either the lawyer was absent on a business trip, or the builder was dallying with the documents.

Frustrated by the entire situation, we understood that we were cheated and made an attempt to cancel the deal and get our money back. This did not happen, and therefore we filed a complaint with the prosecutor's office for fraud. An investigation procedure was initiated. It turned out that the lawyer in question had cheated a number of other people as well. The procedure was really slow, and the outlook for getting the money back looked almost impossible.

Somewhere around that time, I began to practice what I had learned at the Silva UltraMind ESP System workshop. I decided to be very persistent, and every day I visualized the scene where the lawyer transferred the money to my parents' bank account. José Silva said that we should "program in the future in a past-tense sense," so I visualized that the money had already been transferred back to my parents. I told myself that it was best for all the parties involved, and I knew that was the truth.

About three months after I had first taken the Silva UltraMind course, I attended it again to refresh and reaffirm my knowledge. Then I shared what I was doing with Milen Mihaylov, and said I had been doing it every day for over a month. I was wondering how long I should continue to obtain the expected result.

Milen Mihaylov told me that I was visualizing the solution of the problem every day, and this way I was not giving higher intelligence the opportunity to answer. He also advised me if there was any development on this case, I should incorporate the new developments into my visualizations.

So I did what he recommended. Shortly thereafter, the court cases against the lawyer began. Then the lawyer called me and voluntarily asked to transfer half the amount in order to terminate the case and avoid a conviction. He promised that in two months he would return the other half as well.

He did return the first half of the money, but not the rest. Around this time the last case came to an end, and the court imposed a sentence on the lawyer—time in jail. Frightened by his conviction, his relatives made the necessary arrangements in a hurry and in two days asked to pay my parents the rest of the money so that the sentence could be reduced.

Fact: A year and a half after my participation in the workshop and with the use of the lessons learned, the entire amount was transferred to our bank account. I am grateful to José Silva for creating this wonderful system and to my instructor in Bulgaria, Milen Mihaylov, for his readiness to support me and be there for me.

Collecting a Debt

There is another technique that the lady in Bulgaria didn't know about, because it is not included in the UltraMind ESP System seminar. José Silva used to include it in an advanced course he taught to Silva Mind Control graduates, and many people reported having success with it. Here is how he taught it:

Suppose somebody owes you money, or is cheating you out of something that you have a right to, and they know they are doing it, but they won't do what they should. Is there some way to program them to fulfill their obligation—to pay what they know they owe you?

We don't control other people mentally at a distance. We all have free will, and we do what we want to do. So José Silva pointed out that the best approach is to program the other person to *want* to do what needs to be done.

If somebody owes you money and they know they owe it to you, this will cause them to feel guilty, and guilt, according to José Silva, is the worst stressor. Their guilt will hurt their health, their relationships, and other aspects of their lives. So the best thing, for them as well as for you, is to work out a fair and equitable resolution to the problem that is causing their guilt—to pay what they owe you.

If they don't have the money, then maybe there is a creative solution that will be beneficial for both of you. Perhaps they have something they can give you, or maybe there is something they can do for you that you would consider satisfactory repayment.

To get the process started, you can use this technique:

You begin by using the Best Time to Program technique (explained below). When you are in bed and ready to go to sleep, sit up in bed, enter your level and program yourself to wake up automatically at the best time to program. Remain at your level, lie down, and go to sleep.

The first time you wake up during the night or in the morning, sit up in bed, enter your level, and use the Three Scenes Technique.

In the first scene, directly in front of you, visualize the person who owes you money, who has money, but does not want to pay you.

In the second scene, 15 degrees to the left of the first scene, imagine that person drinking any kind of fluid: coffee, soft drinks, water, beer, etc., and thinking of you and about the money owed to you. From then on, every time that person drinks fluid, the memory of the debt owed to you becomes stronger and stronger in the debtor's mind, until it can be tolerated no longer. In order to be relieved of these thoughts, the person will pay you.

In the third scene, again 15 degrees to the left of the second scene, imagine having received the money.

You should always try to solve the problem yourself, but when you are not able to solve it, then you can use the MentalVideo to ask for help from higher intelligence.

And of course remember the Laws of Programming. If you try to use this for purely selfish purposes, it will backfire on you, and eventually you will regret it.

Improving Relationships

Here is a technique you can use to work on relationship problems.

When you need to work on a relationship problem, go to your center with the 3 to 1 Method, and project an image of the person that you desire to communicate with onto your mental screen. We will refer to this person as the *subject*. You can communicate with the subject subjectively while at your center.

You can improve your mental image of the person by recalling the subject's face and facial features: the hair, eyes, eyebrows, nose, cheeks, the character of the face.

Then recall details of the relationship that you have with this subject. Recall some recent interaction. Perhaps there is something about the relationship that you would like to improve. Perhaps there is a future interaction that you want to go smoothly.

You can ask questions of the subject in order to learn more about what they think of the relationship. You can ask what they want to receive from the relationship, and what they are willing to contribute to the relationship.

You can communicate subjectively with words, and even more effectively with mental pictures. The conversations that you imagine between you and the subject will help you to create good mental imagery.

To detect information about what the subject is thinking and experiencing, you can imagine that you are superimposing the subject's head over your own, as though you were putting on a helmet. Then you can put yourself in your subject's place, and whatever you feel will reflect the attitudes and feelings of your subject.

While your subject's head is superimposed over your own, you can ask what they think about the relationship. You may ask what they would like to change about the relationship. Then clear your mind for a moment of time by thinking of another topic.

Then bring your attention back to the question that you asked. Whatever impression comes to you immediately after this will indicate the attitudes and feelings of your subject. You will then concentrate in this particular area. (Whenever you put the subject's head over your own, remember to remove it when you have completed your investigation.)

After you have detected your subject's attitudes and feelings, then project an image that reflects the improvements that you desire. You can talk with the subject subjectively in order to help you create the mental images of a beneficial relationship, with everyone's needs being met and everyone happy with the relationship.

You can mentally make any changes that you desire in the relationship, keeping in mind that the solution must be the best for everybody concerned.

You can use the Three Scenes Technique for this. You can work on any relationship in this manner, at any time you desire. An excellent time to do this is in the morning when you first wake up.

Later, when you meet the subject objectively, in the physical world, you can verbally reinforce anything that you told them when you were at your center. They will detect your true feelings and your desire for a relationship that benefits both of you as well as everybody else involved.

But often it is not necessary to use these specific techniques. When you are talking with someone, you can simply desire to be more sensitive to that person, and you will be—provided you have practiced and developed your ability.

The Best Time to Program

You can use the Three Scenes Technique at any time, even when you are meeting with people. Just defocus your vision and use the daydreaming technique that you learned in chapters 7 and 8.

When you need to program for an interaction that will take place later, there is a technique you can use to find the best time to program. Here is what you do:

When you are ready to go to bed and sleep, sit up in bed, or on the edge of the bed. Close your eyes and turn them upwards approximately 20 degrees, lower your head approximately 20 degrees, and enter your level with the 3 to 1 Method.

Once at your level, tell yourself mentally that you want to wake up automatically at the best time to program, and that you are going to wake up automatically at the best time to program.

Remain at your level, lie down, and go to sleep from your level.

You will wake up automatically during the night, or in the morning, at the best time to program.

When you wake up, sit up in bed, or on the edge of the bed, close your eyes and turn them upwards approximately 20 degrees, lower your head approximately 20 degrees, and enter your level. Then you are ready to do your programming.

ESP in the Palm of Your Hand

You can learn to have alpha functioning virtually all the time and can be certain that most of your decisions will be correct ones if you follow a simple formula. José Silva explains how it happens:

> During the day, your brain dips into the alpha level an average of about 30 times per minute. This happens naturally, and it seems to happen for everybody. But the time in alpha is very short, only microseconds. In all, your brain may be in alpha five seconds out of every minute.
>
> It is during these times that people are able to be certain of making good decisions, decisions that will help to correct problems that hurt our planet and the people who inhabit it.
>
> Maybe that is why the average person, who does not know how to function at alpha consciously when desired, is correct only 20 percent of the time.
>
> As you discover when you learn the Silva UltraMind ESP System, at the alpha level you can be correct more often, probably four times out of five.

But it is not always convenient to find a quiet place where you can relax mentally and physically and enter your level.

Fortunately, you can increase your ability to use the alpha level. When you have had experience functioning at alpha consciously while you are mentally and physically relaxed, then you will also increase your ability to function correctly during the day when your brain is primarily at beta.

With practice, you learn to stay at alpha for longer periods of time. You get acquainted with alpha and get a feeling for it. Later on, you can simply evoke the feeling, and you will have alpha functioning regardless of how the brain is functioning. The mental level will be the equivalent of being at 10 cycles per second of brain frequency.

In other words, you are functioning in the mental world as though your brain were on 10 cps, and, because you have found the door and have practiced using it consciously, you get the benefits now of 10-cycle functioning even if your brain is functioning at beta for 55 seconds out of each minute.

An untrained person will receive very little benefit from those 30 brief trips to alpha, but a trained person, one who is accustomed to functioning at that level, will get greater benefit by perceiving more of the message.

When an untrained person gets a flash of insight, he might remember a quarter of it and get only a fraction of the picture. A trained person, accustomed to functioning at alpha consciously, will get more of the picture.

You can stay at alpha consciously for long periods whenever you need to in order to analyze problems from various perspectives and program solutions.

Here is a simple formula to help you develop and use this ability:

First, learn to find the alpha dimension and function there consciously.

Second, use your abilities to help correct problems on the planet, to help make our planet a better place to live.

When you do these two things, you will enjoy prosperity in all areas of your life.

You can use the Little Finger in the Palm of the Hand technique to assist you in developing your alpha functioning in this manner:

At night, before going to sleep, program yourself to awaken automatically at the best time to program. Stay at your center and go to sleep.

The first time you awaken during the night or in the morning, go to your center again, then curl your fingers of either hand inward so that the tip of your little finger touches the palm of your hand. You can use either hand, or both hands if you wish.

Then program yourself so that whenever you touch the palm of either hand with the little finger of that hand, your mind will adjust to a deeper level of awareness for stronger programming and enhanced intuition.

The more you practice going to your center, the more effective this will be. The more you apply it, the more you attempt to correct problems and experience success in your endeavors, the more confidence you will gain, the more faith you will have, and the more successful you will become.

Programming for Instant Rapport

When you desire to pre-program yourself to have instant rapport with someone, proceed as follows:

Enter your level and program yourself to wake up automatically with the Best Time to Program technique.

The first time that you wake up during the night or in the morning, sit up in bed, and enter your level with the 3 to 1 Method.

Then fold the little finger of either hand, or both hands, to touch the palm of your hand. Think about the meeting you are going to have with the person. Tell yourself mentally, "Whenever I fold the little finger of either hand so as to touch the palm of my hand with it, as I am doing now, the person I am meeting with will sense that I am there to help him (or her), and will know that they can trust me."

Mental Broadcasting

When you desire to use the Broadcasting technique, proceed as follows:

Enter your level and program yourself to wake up automatically with the Best Time to Program technique.

The first time that you wake up during the night or in the morning, sit up in bed, and enter your level with the 3 to 1 Method.

At that time, imagine broadcasting your message, and imagine the person or the people you desire to communicate with receiving the message and responding to it.

Mentally picture people responding to your broadcast in as many ways that you can imagine.

Programming for World Peace

José Silva's brother Juan was our director for foreign countries for 20 years, and was the primary one responsible for introducing the course into more than 100 countries.

Back around 1986 he made a trip all the way around the world. Because of his jet lag, he was having trouble sleeping when he got back, so he watched some live news on the television.

President Reagan and Soviet premier Mikhail Gorbachev were meeting at the Reykjavik summit in 1986. "I didn't have to imagine what the two men were doing or what their surroundings were like," he said, "I could see them."

He thought that would be a great time to program them, so he did.

Juan was a great negotiator. As director of all of our foreign operations, he often had to deal with difficult situations, and he did it very well.

That night, after seeing the leaders of the two most powerful nations in the world on live television, he used his skill and experience to project mentally to them, to persuade them to work towards peace, to be honest with each other, to trust each other.

They didn't reach an agreement to eliminate all nuclear weapons, which they had wanted to do, but the meeting did lead to the first treaty to cut strategic nuclear arms significantly, and to eventually even more arms reductions.

A few years later the Soviet Union was dissolved.

A couple of years after that, we all watched live images on television as the Berlin Wall was torn down.

On Juan's next trip to Germany, he visited the rubble that was left of the wall, and he brought back some of the stones that had once made it up. We still have one of those small stones today, a testament to what is possible if only more people will use the faculties that higher intelligence gave us.

There is no way to prove that Juan influenced events, of course. But when you keep seeing coincidences, it begins to seem pretty natural.

There was a song, written by Ed McCurdy, that Pete Seeger and John Denver and others used to sing, with these lyrics:

> Last night I had the strangest dream
> I ever dreamed before
> I dreamed the world had all agreed
> To put an end to war
> I dreamed I saw a mighty room
> The room was filled with men
> And the paper they were signing said
> They'd never fight again

That's why we believe in UltraMind. It was always the dream that José Silva had: he believed that together we have the capacity to convert the world into a paradise.

10
Forecasting

Everything begins with a thought. If we know what people are thinking and planning, then we can make predictions about what they are likely to do. Research has demonstrated conclusively that your mind is capable of doing that.

José Silva explained it this way:

The past is composed of materialized thoughts.

The present is the process of materializing thoughts.

The future is composed of conceived thoughts that have not yet been materialized.

Because we can always change our minds before we act on our plans, predicting the future is an inexact science. This is actually a good thing, because it gives us an opportunity to change the future. Think of it this way:

Suppose there is a car stalled on the railroad tracks. There is a train 25 miles away that is coming down the tracks at 50 miles an hour. It is easy to predict what is going to happen in half an hour.

But now that we have this information, there are several steps we could take to change the future. We could get some help and push the car off the tracks. We could signal the train to slow down. We could switch the train onto a different track. We could do all three.

The ability to use ESP to detect what is being planned can greatly increase the probability that you will more often be right than wrong in your decision making. Imagine how this can affect your business success. Indeed, as we mentioned earlier, Professor John Mihalasky conducted extensive research showing that, as he puts it, "There is now evidence to suggest that the successful 'hunch player'—a person who makes decisions based on hunches rather than fact or evidence—may have something more solid going for him or her than the odds of chance." For the full details of Professor Mihalasky's study, see appendix C.

The Little Toy Truck

José Silva conducted his own precognition experiment with two of his young research subjects. Initially he wanted to know if thoughts are real and can be detected by somebody else. His results gave him even more information and insight than he had originally sought. Here is what happened.

This experiment involved two children. Let's call them Timmy and Jimmy. Both children were in separate rooms, one with Mr. Silva, the other with another researcher.

Mr. Silva asked Timmy to create something with his mind. Timmy said, "I'm creating a toy truck." When Mr. Silva asked Timmy what it looked like, he replied, "I am going to paint it green, with red wheels."

Meanwhile, in another room, Jimmy went to alpha and was asked to mentally go to the room where Timmy was. After a moment, the researcher asked Jimmy what Timmy was doing.

Jimmy said that Timmy was creating a toy truck. "What does it look like?" "He is going to paint it green, with red wheels."

At the alpha level, Jimmy had not only detected Timmy's thoughts, he had also accurately detected Timmy's intentions. He discovered what Timmy was planning to do.

While we may not be able to know precisely what will happen in the future, we can still make good forecasts by going to level and determining the best thing to do. That's what Rafael Flores, a Silva graduate in Laredo, did.

Intuition Reveals the Perfect Bid

Rafael Flores used his intuition the way he learned in the Silva training to determine how much he should bid to purchase a repossessed house.

He had learned, through practice, that he could rely on the information he detected while at the alpha level, and he trusted the impressions he got this time.

He bid $61,280. The high bid was about $5000 more. Flores was not concerned. Even when the high bidder paid the money for the binder, Flores was not concerned.

A week later, the high bidder defaulted, and Flores got the house. He had programmed to bid the *right* amount, not the *highest* amount, and as a result, he saved several thousand dollars.

The Mexican Lottery Project

José Silva found a unique way to conduct a lot of precognition research in a short period of time without spending much money. He had his young research subjects predict what numbers would come up in the Mexican lottery. He explains:

> We experimented for two years trying to get a prize. I would project a child clairvoyant into the future one day, one week, one month, and up to six months, to the day and time that we knew the lottery was being conducted. The Mexican lottery is conducted three times a week, on Monday, Wednesday, and Friday each week.
>
> When I had them project ahead to the day, date, and time, the child clairvoyants would confirm being right there, observing the numbers that were getting the big prizes. Every time I ran these experiments, I would make a note of the time, the day, date, month, year, whether it was cloudy or sunny, in what direction the wind was blowing, the temperature, the barometric pressure, and what phase the moon happened to be in. We also took into consideration the position the child clairvoyant was in relative to the North or South Pole when he was projecting.
>
> We had made an agreement with the lottery agency to provide us with lists of winning numbers three times a week, and this went on for two years.
>
> The results of this research were that we were occasionally accurate predicting the five-digit numbers that would get the big prize money, but were always wrong on the target time.
>
> No matter what changes we made in the procedure, we were not able to correlate the time factor between the objective

and the subjective dimensions. We were correct on target information but wrong on target time so often that we eventually gave up on the Mexican lottery project.

Nelda and the 50 Tractors

Here is a story from Silva instructor Nelda Sheets about a time when she used precognition to obtain information in order to help her employer make a major business decision, in her own words:

When you practice using your intuition enough, you learn to recognize that special feeling of being right. José Silva referred to this as an emotional feeling.

I was the office manager and a salesperson for a John Deere dealership. My boss and I had taken the Silva training together and used it for such things as mentally encouraging people to pay their bills. If we reached a certain sales quota, we'd win a trip to Nassau in the Bahamas. Our goal was 50 tractors.

When it was time to place our next order, my boss and I worked a case to determine what kind of tractors our customers would need. Normally I was the orientologist, but this time he was. I was the psychic. I went to level and asked how many diesel tractors we should order but was interrupted by a sign on my mental screen flashing the words "order all 50 tractors now" over and over. I told Gene, my boss, and he tried to talk me out of it. (We normally ordered five tractors at a time.) Gene had another concern: our bank balance.

I took a deep breath, relaxed, and did some deepening exercises to make sure I was at a good, deep level. I mentally asked the question again. In response, I got the same neon sign flashing, telling me to order all 50 tractors. This time, I got that familiar feeling that I was right. I knew I was right, and I told Gene. This time Gene agreed, mainly because he knew about a tax incentive he could get if he had tractors in stock.

We ordered all 50 tractors. The John Deere people called me, thinking it was a mistake, since we always order just five at a time. The tractors were delivered, but our lot would only hold five! We had tractors parked in every empty space we could find. The local paper even came to do a story on us.

About a week later we got a call from the John Deere office saying that their workers had gone on strike and that no more equipment would be available. We had our tractors, and we sold all 50. And we enjoyed Nassau.

11

Common Business Situations and Solutions

In this chapter we will cover more ways that you can use what you have learned in the Silva UltraMind ESP System to help you solve common business problems, and to help your business run more smoothly.

As you continue to use the Silva UltraMind techniques, you will find many more ways to apply them. We would love to hear from you about how these techniques benefit you. You are also welcome to contact us with questions or for help. Please see Appendix D for contact information.

Closing a Negotiation

Ed Bernd Jr. took the Silva Mind Control course to help his weightlifting. When he saw the value of the course, he shifted his attention to mental training rather than physical culture. When he came to work at Silva headquarters in Laredo a few years later, he wanted to use his knowledge of weight training to produce a specialized audio workshop on that subject.

Mr. Silva agreed. He had been an athlete when he was young. He had learned to box so that he could defend himself, and was good enough to fight professionally in clubs around South Texas. So he was happy to help Ed with what they called the Silva Star Athlete Program.

They negotiated an agreement whereby Ed would produce the audiotapes and pay Mr. Silva a royalty on all the sales he made. This was the first time that Mr. Silva had relinquished control over his coursework to somebody else, so they worked on the agreement for a couple of weeks until they were both satisfied with it.

"I didn't try to get all that I could," Ed recalled, "but to do what I thought was fair and to respect him and all the work and money he had invested in his system. He seemed to appreciate this. He even made a change that was in my favor!"

After making one final change that Mr. Silva requested, Ed left a copy of the agreement on Mr. Silva's desk, assuming that he would call him in to sign it when he had time. But nothing happened for several days.

"I was eager to get started," Ed recalled, "but I wasn't sure if I should push the issue or not. So before going to sleep, I went to level and mentally rehearsed asking Mr. Silva if he was ready to sign the agreement.

"But that's not what happened," Ed continued. "When I saw him the next day, I walked over to him and opened my mouth to ask if he was ready to sign the agreement, and instead, what I heard myself say—much to my surprise—was: 'Are you ready for me to sign the agreement?'

"That wasn't what I intended to say, but I realized immediately that it was the perfect thing to say. It conveyed the respect that I have for him and all the work he did to create his system. I also wondered, 'Where did those words come from?'

"He reacted immediately, asked me if I had the agreement, if I had a pen he could use; it was like he couldn't wait to sign it. To paraphrase a famous line from the classic movie *Casablanca*, that was the beginning of a beautiful relationship."

A Record-Breaking Trip around the World

A. Victor Kovens of Baltimore, Maryland, the owner of a travel agency specializing in group cruises, used the Silva techniques to help him set a world record and gain worldwide publicity.

Here he presents a case study of how he gained priceless publicity by earning entry into the *Guinness Book of World Records* for flying around the world on commercial airlines faster than anybody ever had.

The Silva techniques have made my experiences as a small-business entrepreneur much easier and a lot more enjoyable. I use the alpha level daily to analyze problems and make decisions, and the more I practice, the more often I make the right decision.

I first took the Silva course in 1974. The following year I made it into the *Guinness Book of World Records* by flying around the world on commercial airlines in less time than anybody had ever done before.

It took me just 47 hours, 48 minutes, and 7 seconds to complete the 25,000-mile trip. I crossed the equator twice, landed in nine countries, and touched points exactly 180 degrees opposite each other on the globe: Lima, Peru, and Bangkok, Thailand.

I visualized and used mental projection to smooth the way. Every step went just as I programmed it. It was almost as though people were waiting for me, like they had been prepared by my mental projection and were ready to help me continue my record-setting journey. This made getting through customs easy.

Making all of the connections from one flight to the next wasn't a problem either. I started in Lima and flew to Bogotá, Caracas, Madrid, Rome, Bangkok, Hong Kong, Tokyo, Los Angeles, and back to Lima.

After the flight, I visualized getting into the record book. I think that was the most important thing. When I was in Los Angeles, I called the book's editor in London to ask him whether I should continue on, and he told me to continue. Before calling, I entered my level and imagined the telephone conversation. When we talked, the editor used the exact words I imagined he would!

When I was back on the airplane for the last leg of the trip, back to Lima, the pilot invited me to sit in the cockpit. He asked me which direction I wanted to land in Lima. I told him to land whichever way he thought was fastest and best.

What was the secret of my programming success? One of the most important elements was the feelings that I incorporated into my programming. Every time I was at my level programming, I thought about how I would feel if I were already in the *Guinness Book of World Records*. I imagined seeing my name in the book and made it so real that I could actually feel the pride and sense of accomplishment seeing my name there.

There were some problems to overcome. For example, one

flight was an hour late because the pilot had to fly an extra 600 miles around Vietnam out of fear of being shot down. I just kept programming and projecting, and it worked. The project was a big success.

That's not the only way the Silva techniques helped me. In 1979 I followed my intuitive guidance and traveled 240 miles to go on a blind date. My intuitive guidance was correct—my date and I have been happily married for more than 20 years.

The biggest, most important, and most satisfying thing I've done in Silva, though, was to help organize a class for homeless people in my hometown of Baltimore. After completing the class, these homeless people had a 70 percent success rate in finding homes or jobs within one week!

Through the years, I have learned the value of going to my level every day in order to make better decisions in my business and personal life, and to get the guidance I need to continue to achieve even more success.

As you can see, there are many, many ways that you can use the creative alpha dimension to help you start and run a small business.

Those of us who operate small businesses seldom have the kind of support that large corporations can afford. That makes it all the more important that we nurture our "invisible means of support," as José Silva called it.

There is plenty of information available to help you meet every challenge, and you can use your mind to retrieve that information, no matter where it is.

And as long as you are doing what you were sent here to do, you will find it easy to get help from higher intelligence to keep you moving along at a rapid pace.

Clairvoyant Employees Are a Good Investment

ESP training for employees can be an excellent investment for businesses. Silva students practice in order to develop their abilities, and since they spend half of their waking day on the job, they often use the techniques to solve job-related problems.

That is one of the things that Razi Anis Contractor of San Antonio, Texas, did. Razi admitted, "It took time for me to start getting results after I took the course in India in 2013, but once I started getting them, I have never looked back."

Razi said that he continues to go to the alpha level two or three times a day but no longer has to use the countdown routine. "Now I just close my eyes and I am already at my deep level," he said.

He programs to correct a wide variety of problems in a way that helps himself and others at the same time. "I do more than five healing cases every day," he said, "and for most of them I am accurate in detecting the problem. I am confident that my programming helps many of those people."

His programming on the job takes several forms. While working at a restaurant in San Antonio, he programmed to help the restaurant prosper and to provide better service to the patrons. "I visualized the parking lot filling with cars, and the restaurant filling with customers," he explained. "I was often able to predict how many customers we would have, and what food they would order.

"For taking orders, when I used to go to them I was able to predict the food they would order in advance. Whatever I have achieved and continue to achieve is only because of my positive attitude and regular practice.

"If you were to ask me how you can learn to do what I do, I would tell you that you now hold in your hands the best mind training system in the world. All you need to do to improve your life and the lives of others, including the mother earth, is to use it on a regular basis.

"I would encourage all employers to give a copy of this book to each of their employees."

Programming for Business Success

Here is how you can program to succeed in business and acquire the material resources that you need, because we all have needs for money. Money is the fuel that keeps the machinery going.

"If you want to do great things," José Silva told us, "you must have a lot of money to do them with. If you have little things to do in life, you don't need too much money to do whatever that is. So the bigger your plans are—meaning, the more people who will benefit—the more help you will get from higher intelligence."

He also emphasized: "Don't ever ask for more than what you need, but do ask for no less than what you need."

When you desire to program to improve your employment or business or financial situation, begin by going to your center with the 3 to 1 Method and analyzing your situation.

Is the work that you are doing helping to improve conditions on the planet?

How many people benefit from your activities?

Is this the best work that you can do toward improving conditions on the planet?

José Silva said that when he needed more money, he would go to his center—the alpha level—and think about how he could provide greater service, or a new product, and would keep in mind what his own needs were, plus a little bit more.

When you have determined what your right work is, and how to go about doing it, then you can program for the kind of business relationships that will help you to accomplish your work.

The alpha brain-wave level is the ideal level for thinking, planning, and making decisions. From your center, you have access to more of the information that is impressed on your own brain neurons. When you are at your center, you can also detect information that has been impressed on other people's neurons.

Always keep the Laws of Programming in mind, and remember that the solution must be the best for everybody concerned.

12

Expert Advice Whenever You Need It

In chapter 7 we mentioned how the biggest oil field in South Texas was discovered near Laredo with the help of dowsing rods. Dowsing rods react to what your mind detects. Your mind influences your brain to send a signal to your muscles and this is what makes the rods move.

When José Silva was conducting his research in the 1960s, he wondered just how far we could go in using the mind to detect information, so he set up an oil exploration experiment with his young research subjects. Here is his report on that research, in his own words:

> We used our trained child clairvoyants for oil exploration. We went to some existing oil fields and took photographs in black-and-white and in color of the oil pumping rigs. We also took the well numbers, and collected some samples of the crude oil from some of the wells.

Then we had the child clairvoyants look at the pictures, and we gave them soda-pop bottles half-filled with crude oil. They were to study the pictures, seeing them at different distances, looking at a picture of a particular well when the picture is upright, at an angle, on the side, and upside down. In other words, they were to rotate the picture setting so that the picture would complete a full revolution, first counterclockwise, then clockwise. We would do this with the black-and-white picture first, then the color picture.

We would write all the data down, such as the position of the child clairvoyant in relation to the magnetic North Pole, the outdoor temperature, the inside temperature, the time of day, barometric pressure, whether it was partly cloudy, cloudy, or sunny, the direction of the wind, and the phase of the moon. All of this data we called "environment information," and we registered it while the child was recording information about the picture of a particular well.

The child would then take the soda-pop bottle, remove the cork, drop some of the crude oil on his fingers, feel it first with his eyes open and then with eyes closed. Then the child clairvoyant would smell the oil, first with eyes open, then with eyes closed. After that, he would taste it by putting some of the crude oil on a finger and touching the tip of his tongue. Again, all this was done first with eyes open, then with eyes closed.

After all this was done, and when the child clairvoyant was called to work the project, which we called a "case," all of the environmental information was noted again just before starting to work the case. Here is how the case would be worked:

Each well had a number, so we identified the case by well

number. The first case was worked by a nine-year-old girl. She was told to enter her level of concentration where she could function clairvoyantly, and to let us know when she was ready to continue.

After doing a series of things mentally to enter her clairvoyant level, she let us know she was ready. Then I said, "I am going to count from one to three and cause a sound with my fingers. At that time, you will project yourself mentally to well number 302." I then counted to three, snapped my fingers and said, "Where are you?" The child answered, "I am at well number 302."

"Describe what you see," I told the child clairvoyant. "I am standing right in front and facing the place where the number 302 is," she answered. "There is a pole to my left, and I am standing right up against the plate that has the number 302." It appeared as though the child had projected into a three-dimensional picture. The child was right there.

Next I said to the child, "Do you see that rod that goes down into a pipe in the ground and is connected to the arm that goes up and down?" She answered, "Yes." Then I said, "Can you mentally project into the well and go down to tell me how deep the well is?" Again the child answered, "Yes." I said, "I will now count from one to three and cause a sound with my fingers. At that time, you will project yourself mentally into the well to tell me the depth of this well. One. Two. Three." I snapped my fingers and said, "You are now inside the well. You can now tell me how deep the well is."

The child started to move her head slightly from side to side, so I asked her, "What is happening?" She answered, "I am starting to go down to see how deep this well is." Then she stopped to ask me, "How do I know how deep is deep? I have nothing to measure with."

Then it dawned on me that the pipe came in sections of certain lengths and that these lengths were linked to one another with couplers. So I said to the child, "As you go down mentally into the well, count the couplers. We will then multiply them by the lengths."

She again started to move her head slightly from side to side and at the same time raised her right arm and motioned with her right hand and index fingers as though she were counting something on a wall, while barely moving her lips. "There are 78 couplers, but remember that the first pipe starting at the top is only half as long as the rest of them," she told us. We noted this information.

Next the child said, "The last pipe at the bottom has a lot of holes around it. I thought that down here there would be a lake or pool of oil," she continued. "But, no, there are holes, or crevices all around the bottom of the well. The oil then runs into the crevices and flows down into the center, or bottom, of the well. Then the pump pumps it out."

The next question to the child was, "Can you tell me the quality of the oil in this well? Is it of high, medium, or low quality?"

The child answered, "How do I do that?"

I said, "Any way you can."

The child stretched her right arm out and with the index and middle fingers appeared to be touching something. Then she brought the fingers to her nose and smelled them. She then touched the tip of her tongue as though she were tasting something. After that she brought her hand down and said, "This oil is not good, not bad; I would say it is fair."

My next question was, "How long has this well been in operation?"

Again the child clairvoyant answered, "How do I do that?"

And again I said, "Any way you can."

The child then said, "Take this down: 333 plus 222. Now divide by 9, and that is the number of months that this well has been in operation."

The next question to the child clairvoyant was, "How many barrels per day is this well producing?"

This time she answered, "What is a barrel?"

I said, "A barrel is a metal drum that holds 42 gallons of crude oil. Crude oil," I explained, "is what is pumped out of the ground."

Then she motioned with both hands as though she were holding her hands around a pipe, and moved them up and down while saying, "Up and down, up and down," with the rhythm of the pumping action. Then she told me, "Take this down: 666 plus 444. Multiply by 3 and divide by 12, and that is the number of barrels that this well produces per year. From that, you can figure the barrels per day if you need to know." At the time, that way of figuring did not make any sense to me. I thought she was just making it up.

The day after we worked this project, I went to an abstract company that keeps records of all wells in the area. I got copies of the driller's log and the electrical log of well number 302 from the specific area. Then I took my information to a geologist friend of mine, along with the driller's log and electrical log. I asked my friend, "Can you tell me how close this information is to the information that is on these logs?"

On the depth of the well, he told me this:

"You say you have 78 couplers. The last one has the head that was used to fire, or shoot, the well at the bottom. The pipes used are 30 feet in length, so 78 times 30 is 2340 feet. The log says it is 2325 feet deep. Since the last pipe installed at the surface of this well was supposed to be half the length, this makes it exactly right. Two thousand three hundred and forty feet less 15 feet is 2325 feet, the correct depth of the well."

Next he told me the length of time the well had been in operation. According to the log, and going by the date when the well had been completed, it figured to five years and four months. The child clairvoyant's figures of 222 plus 333 came to 555, divided by nine equals 61.666 months, compared to five years and four months, or 64 months. The 2.334 months' difference was explained to be in the child clairvoyant's favor because the date on the driller's log was the completion date, and the figures of the child were for time in operation.

The geologist explained, "The well being completed means the drilling, but sometimes it takes months to install the pump. When the pump starts, that is the beginning date of the operation. So the child could have been exactly right as to how long the well had been in operation."

Next came the amount of barrels produced per day. The driller's log indicated 11 barrels per day, or 4,015 per year. The figures the child gave were 666 and 444, which equals 1110. Multiply by three and you get 3330, which comes out to 9.123 barrels per day. The driller's log figures were 4,015 barrels per year, or 11 barrels per day. The child's figures were lower. The geologist said, "It is expected for wells to decrease their barrels-per-day output as the years go by, so there could have been a decrease in production of 1.877 barrels per day in a little more than five years. Again, the child clairvoyant could have been exactly right."

The last thing was the quality of the oil of well 302. The geologist said, "We measure quality by gravity, and to you gravity may mean nothing, so I will interpret for you. According to the gravity indicated on the driller's log, it means that the quality is not good, not bad; it is fair." The geologist used exactly the same words used by the child clairvoyant to explain the quality of the oil of well 302.

When I asked about the crevices that the child mentioned at the bottom of the well, the geologist said that in Texas, to start some wells, drillers use an instrument that holds bullets that are discharged at the bottom of the well. This is the reason for the crevices.

We did many projects such as this, hoping that we would get so good that later a child clairvoyant could be trained to tell us what the drillers were going to find before they drilled. Once they were good at this, they could be trained to tell the drillers where to drill and what they were going to find: the quantity, quality, and depth where the oil would be found.

Child clairvoyants can be trained not only for oil projects, but to detect anything hidden anywhere. Knowing that this can be done is why I like what Luke wrote in the New Testament. Luke reports that Christ said, "But there is nothing concealed that will not be disclosed, and nothing hidden that will not be made known" (Luke 12:2).

Another geologist, also a friend of mine, heard about this research and wanted to know more about it. We had long talks on the subject, and he finally decided to find interested parties to go along with our ideas. My geologist friend found three companies that were interested. We were not to charge for our services until we had proven our point. This was our agreement.

The companies gave us a map to start working. The map covered a section of land 40 miles wide by 70 miles long. The companies were to buy the oil leases from the owners of this land, and we were not to divulge this information, because if land owners became aware that someone had an interest in their land, they would raise the price of the leases.

We started charting the terrain, dividing it into sections and numbering the sections. We also started to train more clairvoyants especially for this oil exploration project. We were ready and waiting to be given the signal to go ahead.

Eventually we did set up a project with an oil company, and gave them locations to drill. The agreement was that they would let us review their data so we could analyze it and improve our methods of determining where to find oil. But they never showed us any data; they just told us that they never found any oil. If that had been true, I suspect they would have been happy to show us the data. But the oil business is so competitive, that whenever they get a competitive advantage, they keep quiet about it.

Uri Geller, the Israeli psychic, is a Silva graduate, and was the featured speaker at one of our annual conventions here in Laredo. He told us that oil companies periodically pay him to let them fly him over potential oil fields and point out where he thinks they should drill. They never tell him if he is accurate or not. But he said they keep coming back to do it again and again.

How to See Your Thoughts

Dowsing rods and pendulums are a great way to see your thoughts in action, but you don't need to travel to the actual location to dowse for oil or silver or gold. You can use a map and let the dowsing rods or pendulum guide you to what you are seeking.

To make a set of dowsing rods, get a couple of pieces of stiff wire, like a wire coat hanger, and bend them into an L shape. Hold the short ends loosely, one rod in each hand, and point the long ends straight ahead. Keep in mind what you are looking for as you walk around or move them around over different areas of a map. It is like daydreaming about what you are looking for. When the rods move towards each other or away from each other, that is an indication that your mind has detected what you are looking for.

"Water witches" use a forked stick or divining rod the same way when they search for a spot to drill a water well. They often use a willow twig for this. When they get near water, the willow twig points down toward the ground where the water is.

You can make a pendulum by hanging any small, weighted object at the end of a short chain. Many people like to use a crystal at the end of the chain. You can hold one end of the chain, with the crystal at the other end, and "calibrate" it by asking it to show you "Yes," "No," "Maybe," and "I don't know." There are four different ways the crystal can move: side to side, forward and back, clockwise, and counterclockwise.

Once you know what each movement means, then you can ask it questions and allow it to move in one of those four directions.

Our good friend Raymon Grace is a former Silva instructor, an author, lecturer, and an expert in dowsing. Here is what he has to say:

Dowsing is a way to enhance ESP, as is observing the physical movement of a pendulum to confirm what we already know. You can use a pendulum to confirm what you already know through your natural ESP, but don't believe you know it.

The terms "ESP" and "dowsing" are somewhat interchangeable. Perhaps it would be fair to say that dowsing is training wheels for ESP.

One of our earlier success stories was with my friend, businessman Jeff Jones. Jeff's company needed some equipment that had to be custom-made. The tools to make this equipment also had to be custom-made and were not available in the marketplace.

Jeff and I had a hunch that the tools had been made by another company but were not in use. By using ESP and dowsing, we found the tools in a warehouse in another state, and Jeff bought them for 15 percent of their value, saving $300,000.

Another success involved my brother David. He was chief photographer for a newspaper that downsized, and he needed another job. I programmed for him, and within 20 minutes he was offered a job with a real estate company.

Here is David's statement of what happened.

"The real estate license itself is a 90-hour class, so I needed a month to complete the class. With all the paperwork and filings it took about 35 days. The Virginia license did take a little over a week to get the paperwork in."

His first sale was over half a million dollars, and he is now the leading salesperson in the company.

My friend John owns a real estate company in the Midwest, and I help him with problems that arise when dealing with selling houses. Here is how:

He sends me a list of the houses, and with ESP I check the houses and the people to see where the problems are—and then I correct the problems mentally.

The use of ESP, intuition, gut feeling and/or dowsing has helped my friends and me solve problems for years.

We also made money doing it.

For more information on Raymon Grace, visit www.raymon-grace.us.

Free Advice from Experts

The alpha brain-wave level is the ideal level for thinking, planning, and making decisions. From your center, you have access to more of the information that is impressed on your own brain neurons. When you are at your center, you can also detect information that has been impressed on other people's brains.

You can do more than detect the information that has been impressed on other people's brains: you can also detect how they used that information, and the results that they got.

This means that you have the ability to learn from other people's experiences and use their experiences as if they were your own.

This is wisdom.

To detect information that is impressed on someone else's brain neurons, invite them to join you while you are at your center. Proceed in the following manner:

Go to your center with the 3 to 1 Method. Once at your center, project an image of the expert on your mental screen. You can invite a specialist in advertising, for instance, or marketing, and ask how they would market your product or service. You can invite a legislator and ask what changes there will be in laws this year. You can invite a career counselor and seek ideas.

You can use this technique to consult with an expert in any field, so that you will have access to all of the knowledge and experiences that this expert has.

Once you have decided which expert you want to consult with, then project an image of the expert onto your mental screen. Recall the expert's face. Then ask whatever you like. Clear your mind for a moment of time by thinking of something else. Then start thinking again to figure out the answer. The thoughts that come to you are that person's thoughts.

It may feel as if you are making it up. It may feel as if you are putting words in the expert's mouth, as if it is your answer, not the expert's. That is the correct feeling. Accept it.

You can use this technique to consult with a prospect, customer, or client, to help you understand their situation better, so that you will be able to serve them better by making the best recommendations for them.

You may create a duplicate of your leading competitor, of a top attorney, of a high-priced market consultant, of a government expert, of a religious leader, even of a historical figure.

You can use this technique to learn what other people are planning so that you can protect your business and your customers. This way you can make sure they always have all of the information that they need in order to make the best decisions about what to buy and whom to buy it from.

You can talk with this expert at any time, and imagine the advice that this person would give you regarding any question or any situation.

The only real difficulty is remembering that we can do this. We plow ahead, forgetting that we can ask an expert.

Always keep the Laws of Programming in mind, and remember that the solution must be the best for everybody concerned, and be sure to thank the expert before coming out of your level.

Creating a Master Painter

One day at a meeting of a group of artists who had taken the course with José Silva in Amarillo, Texas, he was asked, "What else can we use clairvoyance for?" He answered, "For doing everything that is constructive and creative in a better way." The next question was, "Can we use it for painting better, and how?" He said, "I will show you a way right now."

Here is his report, in his own words, on the exciting demonstration that came next:

There were about 45 graduates in this meeting, but Mr. Fitz, the art professor, was not present, so I selected a woman sitting in the front row. "Madam," I said, "will you come forward and sit in this chair?" She came and sat in the chair at the front of the room, facing everybody. I then told this woman to enter her level, because I wanted to talk to her at her level.

When she indicated she was at her level, I said, "What is your name?" The answer was "Mrs. F." I then continued, "Mrs. F., who do you like to paint like?" Mrs. F. answered, "Like Van Gogh." I then asked Mrs. F., "Have you read Van Gogh's biography?" She answered, "Yes." I continued, "Mrs. F., since you are a painter, you must have good visualization and good imagination. Could you, using your visualization and imagination, create a copy of Van Gogh here at your level?" Mrs. F. answered, "You mean something like making believe?" I said, "Yes." Mrs. F. said, "Yes, I can do that."

I then told Mrs. F. to start creating a copy of Van Gogh, starting with the head, on down to the feet. Mrs. F. started motioning with her hands as though she were sculpturing a body on her right, starting with the head. Everybody in the room was watching Mrs. F. create her Van Gogh at her level of clairvoyance.

When Mrs. F. finished, I told her that from now on, when she would be painting out of level, and she needed to ask Van Gogh a question about a painting problem, all she had to do was bring the tips of the first three fingers of either hand together, concentrate on the image of Van Gogh she had created, and ask the question mentally. After that, whatever ideas came to her would be Van Gogh's answer.

"Now come out of your level and paint something for us with this new concept," I told her. Mrs. F. came out of her level and set up her easel, canvas, pigments, and brushes. Occasionally while painting, Mrs. F. would bring together the tips of the first three fingers of her left hand, or sometimes of her right hand, and concentrate a little, then continue painting. When Mrs. F. finished her painting project, a vase with flowers in it, everybody appeared amazed at the finished product and how she went about doing it. Without realizing it, I had selected a person who had had only a few lessons in art.

At that time, Mr. Fitz arrived and wanted to know why there was such a commotion. When he heard what had taken place, he told everybody to sit down and that he would study the painting. Mr. Fitz then analyzed the painting from top to bottom, pointing out the similarities to a Van Gogh. When he had finished explaining what he detected in the painting, Mr. Fitz even had me convinced that there was something of Van Gogh in it.

When I went back to Amarillo a month later, I was met by a group of painters who had witnessed the Van Gogh experiment and who now wanted to create their own Rembrandt, Da Vinci, Michelangelo, or other masters. We did just that, creating a master for each who wanted one.

Three months later, this same group wanted to meet with me again. When we met, they said they wanted to let me know that they had decided to continue being their own personal selves, that they did not want to be copies of anybody. I then explained to them that there was nothing wrong with starting their painting profession as copies of the great masters. "In other words," I told them, "picking up where the great masters stopped." The group appeared to have liked and accepted the explanation.

The Mental Mentor

Here is one more technique you can use to get guidance and motivation any time you need it: you can create a mental duplicate of a person you admire and call on this person any time you need someone to encourage you and remind you to do the things you know how to do. We call this person your *Mental Mentor.*

Your Mental Mentor can be anyone you choose. It can be a living person, or someone who has passed on. It can be someone you knew long ago, or somebody you have only read about or seen on television. You can choose anyone you like.

To create your Mental Mentor, enter your level, and once at your level, think of a person that you admire, someone who has helped you and taught you and guided you in your life or your career, for instance, or someone you know about and admire. You can use your memory of this person as a Mental Mentor.

Create and project onto your Mental Screen a mental picture of this person. Recall what this person looks like: their height and weight, their facial features, the color and length of their hair. Recall how this person moves, their gestures; recall how this person talks. Now imagine your Mental Mentor moving away from the Mental Screen and becoming dynamic and fully alive.

This mental duplicate that you have created will be known as your Mental Mentor.

You can imagine talking with your Mental Mentor at any time, and imagine how your mentor would guide you and support you and serve as an example for you.

Your Mental Mentor can encourage you when you are performing tasks. Simply recall your mentor, imagine what he or she would say to you, and use this to help you achieve greater results.

13
Triggering Creative Ideas

Management and creativity are two very different mind-sets, but they can coexist and help you achieve greater business success than can either one alone. Here is an example of how a business manager assembled and managed a team of creative people to implement an idea he had that turned out very well.

Lee Iacocca had an idea back in 1960, and trusted his hunch. He thought that young adults would love a new American car model based on European styling, with sports car handling and a powerful engine, as long as the price was reasonable.

He assembled a team of the best creative people he could find to design the legendary Ford Mustang automobile. Ideas aren't worth anything until they are expressed in the physical world.

Iacocca was remarkable in that he understood creative people and their spontaneity well enough to let them produce their best work, and he understood managers and their need to control events in order to succeed in business. As a result, he was able to complete the project and do it in record time with a remarkably small budget. The Ford Mustang became the best-selling car for the company since Henry Ford's original Model T.

The creative team included an engineer who suggested they save money and time by building the new car on the Ford Falcon chassis; an account executive at their ad agency who compiled a list of names, including *Mustang*; and another ad agency executive, who got the car on the cover of *Time* and *Newsweek* the same week. Neither magazine had ever shown a retail product on the cover before then. Then of course there were the engineers and designers who created the car and the marketing campaign.

Iacocca had to sell the idea to Henry Ford II, which wasn't easy, since Ford had just taken a $250 million loss with the ill-fated Edsel. He wasn't enthusiastic about taking another risk with yet another new and unproven idea. It took several trips to Ford's office, but Iacocca eventually persuaded him to give it a chance.

Microsoft's Bill Gates is a lot like this. He recognizes good ideas when he sees them, he knows how to manage creative people and get the best out of them, and he certainly knows how to manage a business successfully.

In this chapter, we'll take a look at creativity, and how to manage it without repressing it, so that you can use it to help you in all aspects of your career.

Everything that exists was first a thought. Mind guides brain, and brain guides body. Whatever you can conceive and believe, you can achieve.

One of the first people to use the Silva system for inventive purposes was José Silva's brother Juan. They wanted to see if a person who had never had any interest in inventing anything could become an inventor by using the alpha level and the techniques that José Silva was developing.

They reasoned that if Juan could do it, then anybody could.

Here is Juan's story.

Inventing an Inventor

Juan Silva worked side by side with his brother José during their research. They wanted to see if they could use the alpha level to help them invent something that could be of value.

They were extremely successful at it. Juan said that all José did was to program him to have a desire to invent something that would be of some benefit.

The result was that he invented a vending machine. He sold the patent to a company in Mexico, and agreed to go to work for the company to set up and supervise the production of the machine. Juan stayed on that job for more than a decade.

In addition to running the factory, he was also teaching people the Silva techniques in his spare time. He considered those years to be the best of his life.

Here is a transcript of what Juan told us about the creative process that he used.

I told José that I would take part in this experiment on one condition: that he refer to me as a research subject, and not call me a guinea pig.

You program yourself to accomplish a particular feat, shall we say the assembly of a mechanism.

You don't know what you are supposed to do about it, so you program yourself.

You are not going to get a direct answer to it, a specific answer. No. You are going to dream about related things, and whatever other things that flow intuitively to you about what you are supposed to be doing.

It has always been the case—like with everything else—you are not only supposed to program, not only supposed to imagine, not only supposed to scheme things, you are supposed to execute them too.

You are body-mind. Don't leave your body behind, or your mind behind.

So what you programmed for, and what you dreamed about, if anything, really doesn't make any sense. But when you start fiddling around, trying to work or draw whatever you think, this is when it starts flowing, when the information starts flowing.

All of a sudden you will start to accomplish what you need.

You might not recall dreaming about a rack gear. You start thinking, "Where can I put a rack gear? I've heard of round gears, square ones, but rack gear? Where did this come from?"

I'm telling you this because this is what happened to me.

Consequently, when I went back to work on this rack, as to how I was going to use it, it was obvious it was going to have to be with gravity, and was going to have to be perpendicular to something.

So one thing will lead to another.

But you must execute.

If you just leave it and write it down, what you dream about, and leave it right there, it's not going to go any further.

So whatever you program for, make sure you execute, carry it out. It's always the case. You have to get your body and mind together, to work.

So this invention of mine came about like that. Then I needed a coin mechanism. I needed something to detect these coins, within thousandths of an inch and so forth.

I think that the most outstanding thing that happened to me along these lines, when I invented this machine, was the purpose of what I finally wound up with. I never dreamed about the purpose, I never programmed about the purpose of it; I mean, the basic purpose, yes: I wanted to sell sodas, I wanted to sell candies, whatever.

But the fact that there were four different types of coins, and they could coin any one, or any combination of them—they could change the coins, or change the price of the merchandise, and my machine wouldn't become obsolete. I could make adjustments.

Now this is what I didn't dream about. This is what I actually did not program for. And everything came out like that.

This is what's very peculiar and outstanding, that I have never been able to figure out.

You know, it is awfully hard for you to invent something and to set the purpose for what it is supposed to do. But when five other things come up that the machine can do, well, you definitely didn't think about that, you didn't program for that.

So it is just as if somebody took you by the hand and led you, you know, all through all of this programming.

It happened at a low level (brain frequency) of conscious awareness, that I had acquired and had worked on it and had practiced it every day. Every day I would go to my level and practice deepening exercises until I was sure that I had gone below 10 cycles. Then once a week, on Sunday, I would do the complete Long Relaxation Exercise.

So I attribute my programming success to the fact that I was at a lower level of conscious awareness.

Dream Solutions

BREAKTHROUGH FROM A DREAM

Dreams are a source of creative ideas. Humanity has been benefiting from information received in dreams for centuries.

Everybody dreams, but not everybody remembers their dreams. If you don't remember your dreams, you can program yourself to start remembering them. Enter the alpha level when you are ready to go to sleep, program that you want to remember a dream, and you are going to remember a dream.

Once that is successful, you can program yourself to remember your dreams (plural). Then you can program the kind of dreams you want to have. If you have a problem you need to solve, you can program to have a dream that will contain information to help you solve the problem.

That is what the research director at a company that produces biomedical products did shortly after attending the Silva Mind Control course.

Probably the most common problem in business is making the correct decision. José Silva always reminded us that there is no such thing as a problem without a solution. If you have enough information, it is easy to make decisions. If you could tell in advance what the results of your decision would be, imagine how much easier it would be to make decisions.

The research director at a company called New Dimensions in Medicine did not have enough information to complete his project. He had been working hard in the laboratory to come up with a formula for artificial arteries.

Imagine the benefits. At the time, doctors had to transplant arteries from other parts of the patient's body to replace bad arteries in the heart. If they could use artificial arteries, it would be much easier on patients, and would undoubtedly extend their lives in many cases.

Silva instructor Ken Obermeyer explained what was happening with the project:

"He had already developed four new formulas at his beta level," Obermeyer reported. But there was still a problem with the body rejecting the foreign material.

The researcher attended a Silva course. He reasoned that there was nothing to lose, and perhaps something to gain, by programming to have a dream that would contain information for solving the problem he had in mind—the best formula for artificial arteries.

"He awakened during the night," Obermeyer said, "and wrote out a formula." Then he went back to sleep.

"When he awakened in the morning, he saw the formula, went into the laboratory, put a sample together and found that the human body would accept his plastic.

"One interesting note about this creative solution," Obermeyer continued: "The chemist said that if he had considered this formula based on what he knew at the beta level, he wouldn't have believed it to be a formula the body would accept. He would not have come up with this solution through reason and logic."

This is not to say that reason and logic should be ignored, Obermeyer is quick to point out. We all need the logical, objective beta level for analysis and reasoning. We also need the creative and intuitive alpha level for the creative insight that it offers, and for the help and guidance that higher intelligence can provide to us.

This dream turned out to be worth millions of dollars to the company and saved countless lives.

Creative People Think Differently

Creative people think differently from managers. While managers have specific goals and objectives and don't want anything to impede them from gaining them, *creativity* is defined by the *Business Dictionary* as a "mental characteristic that allows a person to think outside of the box, which results in innovative or different approaches to a particular task."

The story of Lee Iacocca and the creation of the Ford Mustang is a great example of how creativity can lead to big profits. But it doesn't happen without management or control. If Iacocca hadn't managed to stay within his budget and within the time constraints placed on him, we wouldn't have the Mustang today.

While management and creativity might require very different mental characteristics, both are valuable, especially in today's innovative—and disruptive—environment.

Here are some thoughts from Ed Bernd Jr. on managing creative people:

Creative people often feel that the conformity and control that are valued in many business environments put a big damper on the spontaneity and expression that creative individuals thrive on.

I went to journalism school, not business school, so I don't know what they teach in business school, but sometimes I think they must teach managers to hide their emotions unless they can be used to provide a business advantage. Creative people don't want to suppress their thoughts and emotions, because this suppresses their creativity.

This can lead to misunderstandings, hurt feelings, and problems. More than once, while listening to one of our company managers, they said something that reminded me of something I should have done but had forgotten about, and I flinched when I remembered it. The executives took it personally and thought it was aimed at them. They didn't even bother to ask me, they just yelled at me and told me to leave. And I did.

Brainstorming is a popular technique with businesspeople for coming up with creative ideas. It is also carefully controlled: you start with a specific objective, and no objections or negative thoughts are permitted.

Obviously brainstorming works, but it doesn't work very well for me. I've had some great ideas come to me after people objected and told me why my idea wouldn't work. For instance:

Several years ago I wanted to create a series of video workshops that would show people many of the ways that they could benefit from the Silva techniques in business to produce more sales, for fitness and sports, and to maintain good relationships.

But I was told that we didn't have money in the budget to cover it, and it was too risky to take a chance on it. There were a lot of employees who depended on getting a paycheck every week, so they weren't willing to risk the money. If I could reduce the cost enough, they would consider it.

I couldn't reduce the production cost and still have a quality product to showcase our benefits. I couldn't reduce the cost to obtain the inventory. So I was stuck. Or was I?

"Suppose I could get somebody to partner with us on this project, to finance it in exchange for a share of the profits?" I asked.

With a look of skepticism, they told me to go ahead and if I found somebody who would agree to that, then I could proceed.

I went to Victor Kovens [the travel agent you met in chapter 11]. Victor was always eager to help whenever he could. He was proud that he had attended every Silva convention for more than 20 years.

He loved the idea and put up the money for it—the equivalent of about four months of my salary. We agreed that we would send all of the revenue from the project to him until we had reimbursed him for all the money he had advanced us, and then we would pay him a percentage of the profits after that.

In less than a year, not only had Victor recovered all of his investment, he had doubled his money. The most meaningful thing to Victor, I think, was that he was able to be a partner in a Silva project.

The project worked out better than if we had financed it ourselves. The combination of Victor's business success, coupled with his many successes with the Silva technique, were a great help to us. We even included him on some of the videos we made, and he encouraged Silva instructors to buy them and use them to help promote the course. It also gave us a new idea we had never considered before for financing projects.

We were doing a lot of programming, especially at night before going to sleep, so maybe higher intelligence noticed and steered us in a different direction by "influencing" somebody to reject our original idea.

If you ask for help with the MentalVideo and don't get what you want, it doesn't mean that higher intelligence didn't hear you—sometimes they hear you and the answer is "no."

As a businessperson, you will benefit if you know the best way to deal with the various people you come into contact with. Some people work better under pressure. Others just shut down when somebody "puts the lid" on their ideas.

You can use the techniques that you are learning in this book to help you know how to deal with these various personality types. This will expand your business opportunities.

At your level, you can imagine talking with people, asking them what they think and how they feel. You can imagine "putting their head on" (as you did in the human anatomy mental projection exercise in chapter 7). As you gain more experience working in the subjective (mental) dimension and using these techniques, it will be more natural to you and will happen automatically.

José Silva seemed to have an instinct for knowing the right thing to do at the right time. Many times he would tell me, "OK, let's see what you come up with." That is like waving a red flag in front of a bull. I take it as a challenge, and it gets my creative juices going.

Other times he would say, "I know you have you own ideas, but let's do it my way this time." It was easy to tell when he was serious, and when he was, I did it his way.

Sometimes we annoyed each other a little bit, but he was a creative person too, and our understanding of each other's needs created an environment where we did a lot of good things together.

The Silva Alpha Think Tank

José Silva developed a technique that you can use when you want to work on a project as a group. He called it the Silva Alpha Think Tank. It doesn't use the same rules as the beta-level think tank that many businesses use. You may find ways to implement this technique that work best for your group. The following is a transcript of José Silva guiding a session in one of his seminars:

This is a group project. The director can sit at the head of the table, and the other participants on each side of the table.

Sit in a circle, in chairs or around a conference table. Everyone goes to level. As each person gets to level, they will say out loud, "I'm at my level." When everyone has said they are at their level, the director will begin.

The director will ask, "Who has a problem you would you like to work on?" After the first person suggests a problem, then the director will go to the next person and ask, "How about you?" The director will ask each person in the group.

Then the members of the group, still at their level, will decide which is the most important problem that they need to work on.

Once they decide on a problem to work on, everyone will work on the problem. They will decide which is the most serious problem, the most important problem to work on.

Each will give advice, suggest what they will do. Each person will mention any ideas that come to them about how to solve the problem.

Then after the members of the group have suggested ideas, and group members have discussed them, they will select the best idea, and they will all work on that idea. After they have agreed on what should be done and the best way to work on the problem, then everybody will use that idea, at the same time, to work on the problem.

A board of directors can work on problems with this technique. The owners of a business can work on problems together with this technique.

14

The Business Leader of the Future

The highway to success is not a straight road.

Success is not for the faint of heart. There are many false starts and adventures that may seem like distractions at the time, obstacles that test our strength and our resolve.

Looking back, we may realize that it was those "failures" that taught us things we needed to know in order to achieve our ultimate purpose, and that in overcoming the most difficult obstacles we built the strength that would be required for future successes.

José Silva's path to success was a long one. Most observers looking at a six-year-old orphan shining shoes on the streets of Laredo back in 1920 would not have given him much of a chance to achieve all that he did.

Yet his life, guided as he was by higher intelligence, provides a blueprint for the leaders of the future. You as a businessperson are in a better position than most to be a good example and to help lead humanity into what José Silva called *the second phase of human evolution on the planet.*

He provided insight into his life in articles he wrote through the years. His life can serve as a guide and as an inspiration as you create your own success story. Here is what he said:

Closing Thoughts from José Silva

Life is often hard, and presents many challenges. Yet we must persist and do what we are supposed to do.

I've certainly had many challenges in my life:

My father died when I was four years old, as the result of a terrorist act during the Mexican revolution.

My mother remarried and moved away, while I stayed with my grandmother.

I never went to school, because I was working to bring in money for the family.

I grew up in a border town in the Southwest, where bullies like to pick on kids as small and as light as I was.

I've been through economic depressions—the Great Depression, which affected the entire United States, and numerous local depressions that result from such things as bad weather, fluctuating oil prices, peso devaluations, and air-base closings.

When I began researching ways to help my children develop more of the natural mental abilities—the research that lead to the development of our system—many of my friends shunned me and my family, they ridiculed us, and they even called the law on us.

My church—which is supposed to offer spiritual support during hard times—threatened to excommunicate me for trying to help people in ways that they didn't understand.

When I completed my research and tried to show the world what I had done, I was rejected by scientists, by the government, and by the educational and religious establishments.

When I set up a business, many of the people I had taught to teach the Silva Method turned on me, took the course that I had spent 22 years and half a million dollars to develop, and began teaching it as their own.

When I told an author that he could write a book that included my copyrighted material and we would split the profits, he walked away and wrote his book with one of the people who had taken my material and was teaching it without my permission. His book was a big seller at the time, but now it is out of print, and our books are still being sold worldwide.

Today I have many loyal people who have stuck with me for two decades or more. Yet I'm still disappointed sometimes when someone I thought was loyal says that I don't know what I'm doing, and goes out to teach on his or her own.

It doesn't make sense sometimes. All I've tried to do my entire life is to correct problems and help people, and to earn enough money by doing so to take care of my own family, so that we don't have to depend on anyone else.

I'm not looking for sympathy. I know that there are people who have had a more difficult life than I have. Everyone has challenges to face.

I was asked what gives me the courage to persist in the face of so many obstacles; how do I know I am doing the right thing; how do I know what I should be doing with my life?

Purpose in Life

My first purpose, when I was six years old, was to take care of myself and my family. Somebody had to earn money, and being the oldest male, I decided I should do it. This is not difficult to figure out. Even animals take care of their own families. There is really nothing special about that.

I have never been able to understand people who don't try to take care of their own families, or divorced fathers who fail to even support their own children. People like that are not acting like human beings; they are not even acting in as ethical a manner as most animals.

Giving Service

In my efforts to support myself and my family, I learned very quickly that people were not willing to give you money simply because you needed it, but would gladly pay you if you gave them something of value, something that solved a problem for them or helped them to enjoy their life more. I solved the problem of dirty shoes by shining their shoes. I sold them newspapers, cleaned their offices, took them shopping, cooked in their restaurants, helped them build buildings.

I found that I could earn even more money by helping more than one person at a time.

For instance, when I sold household items like needles and thread door-to-door, people appreciated my service. When I recruited several more young people to help me take my merchandise door-to-door, I helped even more homeowners, and helped these young people earn some money for their families also. As a result, I earned much more money than before.

The more people you help, the more valuable your services are, and the more money you make.

Did I enjoy doing all that work?

Not particularly.

Was it satisfying?

It is always satisfying to fulfill your obligation to take care of your family. And it made me feel good to know that I was helping people.

Some people always pick jobs that they enjoy. They seem to be compensated by the enjoyment; but if they are not correcting a lot of problems, if they are not helping a lot of people, they will probably not receive a great deal of money.

Some people choose jobs that are very satisfying, because they are helping people in need. Again, they may receive the bulk of their compensation in feelings of satisfaction rather than cash.

Different people have different needs.

My needs were to take care of myself and my family.

And I found that the best way to do that was to help as many people as much as possible.

Eventually, in the 1960s, I was employing crews of workers to install television antennas so that Laredo residents could get good television reception, even from the San Antonio stations 150 miles away.

This was hard work, but I was helping the workers that I employed, as well as helping the people who watched the television after we installed the antennas.

Then I found something that helped a lot more people, and helped them a lot more than any television set ever could: I began teaching people how to use more of their minds to be healthier, luckier, and more successful in life.

Helping Millions of People

The courses that we created from my research findings have helped millions of people, in every way you can imagine.

Our files here at the office are bulging with testimonials and thank-you letters from people who have overcome terminal illnesses, who have learned how to earn all the money they need to support their families, who have overcome challenges and gotten the education that they need, and so much more.

It is interesting that during the 22 years when I was conducting my research, I always had plenty of money for my family and also enough left over to invest in research.

I was actually earning more money than other people in similar businesses, even though they were helping as many people with their business as I was with mine.

Why was this?

I attribute it to the fact that I was committed to helping people with research.

I don't mean involved; I mean committed. Do you know the difference?

The difference in being involved and being committed is like ham and eggs. The chicken was involved; the pig was committed.

I was doing much more than helping my own children.

When other parents saw that my children had started getting better grades, they asked me to help their children. I did so.

When people learned that I could help them with holistic faith-healing techniques, they came to me looking for help. I attempted to help all who came. In fact, my brother Juan and I used to go out looking for people to help.

When other adults in Laredo saw what the children could do, they asked me to teach them my techniques also.

Eventually I was teaching my system to groups of people. I did not do it for money, but to help them. I finally began to accept a small amount from those who came to the meetings to help pay the cost of the room and refreshments.

Help from the Other Side

I believe that higher intelligence—on the other side, as we like to say—guided me in the correct direction because I demonstrated my commitment to use what I learned to help people and correct problems.

Many people get involved and promise a lot of things. I was committed, and I was producing. From the very beginning, I shared everything I was learning with anyone who wanted to know.

How did I know that I was doing the correct thing?

I didn't always know.

Did I ever have doubts?

You bet I did.

Calling It Quits

One time I got so discouraged while reading psychology books late at night after everyone else had gone to bed, that I threw the book across the room and it slid under the sofa. That was it. I had found the help I needed for my children. I was frustrated and ready to quit.

Why should I continue to take the abuse and criticism from people in the community?

Why should I, who had learned to read and write with the help of my sister and brother because I never attended school, try to understand books that college students found difficult?

Why should I continue to put my money into something for other people's benefit?

That's how I felt.

So what caused me to change my mind, to realize that part of my purpose in life was to continue my study and research?

A dream.

I had a very strange dream that same night, a dream that contained numbers. I spent all of the next day trying to figure out what the dream and the numbers meant.

That evening, somebody suggested we look for a lottery ticket with those numbers. In Nuevo Laredo, Mexico, we found the ticket, and it won me $10,000.

Well, I found out what the numbers meant, but what did the dream itself signify?

Later when I was alone, I sat down and thought about everything that had happened, both before and after the dream.

The one thing that stood out, that was different from my normal routine, was my little violent episode when I threw the psychology book across the room and vowed to end my research.

Could there be a connection? Could it be that that book slamming into the wall woke up somebody else besides my wife? Could it have gotten the attention of somebody on the other side, who realized that they needed to send me a sign to let me know I should keep going?

Was that their way of compensating me for the work I was doing?

That was the conclusion that I drew from the episode.

So I went back to work, studying, testing, trying out many different things to see what would work.

A few years later I got discouraged again.

That was when Christ—the symbol of my religion—came to me.

It was actually a picture of Christ that my son Ricardo put into my lap one morning shortly after I had packed all of my books away in the attic. At least this time I wasn't throwing the books around.

Ricardo came running in from the rain and tossed the rolled-up papers to me.

When I picked them up, they were dry. How could that be?

When I unrolled them, the life-sized face of Christ was looking me straight in the eye.

I used to box when I was young, but this experience hit me as hard as any fist has ever hit me. I felt as if he was asking me, "Didn't I tell you to continue your research? Why are you not obeying me?"

I went into the bathroom and locked the door. I didn't want my family to see me cry.

Knowing What's Right

Here are some of the conclusions that I draw from my life experiences:

We have been sent here to help correct problems, in order to make this world a better place to live.

Correcting problems means that we should be doing constructive and creative things. We should not destroy or do anything to make life more difficult for anyone, but should make life better whenever we can.

The more problems we correct, and the more people we help, the more compensation we will receive.

Our helpers on the other side, the helpers that I refer to as higher intelligence, offer us guidance. It is up to us to listen and to heed the guidance.

When you are centered, when you function at the alpha level, you will receive the guidance from the other side. It is not just ideas that count—they might be coming from your own imagination. Notice what happens in the physical world. When things are going well, you are on the right track. If you have too many problems in your life, you may be going in the wrong direction.

I believe that I was one of the fortunate 10 percent of humanity that naturally functions at the 10-cycle alpha brain wave frequency. I was centered. I used those levels naturally, without even realizing it. I was at the correct level, and had the correct attitude—helping people—so I got the messages.

Now you can do the same. Enter your level with the 3 to 1 Method the way you learned in our system. Ask for guidance. If you are sincere, and if you are demonstrating your sincerity by taking action—if you show that you are really committed—then you will be guided to know what is right.

And when that happens, it is easy to press on, to persist, to have faith, to trust, and to do what you know in your heart is right to do.

As it says in the Bible, "If God is with you, then who can be against you?"

A Vision of the Future

On these next pages, I will share with you the vision I see of the future on this planet when all people are functioning clairvoyantly.

Once we train all humanity to be clairvoyant, there will be no more sickness, and no more problems of any kind, because clairvoyants can develop into geniuses capable of solving all kinds of problems. Then and only then, by learning to function with full awareness from the center of our brain frequency spectrum, can we reach perfect balance by using both brain hemispheres to the utmost for thinking.

Then and only then will we change from hurting and killing each other to helping each other, so that all of us together can convert this planet into a paradise. Then and only then will we understand that to function correctly on this planet we must do everything that is good, and that means to supervise the evolving process of creation, caring for the Creator's creation and his creatures. Then and only then will we understand that we should not get involved in doing what is wrong, and that is that we should not hurt the Creator's creation or his creatures, because that would be the real sin.

In business, there will be far more executives who will be able to use clairvoyance to make accurate business decisions by determining the needs of the public ahead of time. Executives will be healthier, and thus more valuable to their companies, because they will use their clairvoyant level to maintain their own good health by relieving stress and relaxing.

Government leaders of all nations will project into the future mentally to detect the needs of their people and be prepared when those needs arise. Government leaders, using their clairvoyance, can sense whether the people they are dealing with are sincere, and also sense what future plans others have. At this time, wars between nations will cease, because the element of surprise will be nil.

Law enforcement agencies will use their mental abilities to help them capture criminals and virtually put crime to an end. On the other side of the issue, people with criminal tendencies will be identified and taught to function in a superior manner that makes it unnecessary to engage in criminal activity to achieve what they desire.

There will be an abundance of natural resources in the world of tomorrow, because petroleum engineers and geologists will use clairvoyance to dowse for minerals—without using a divining rod. They will learn to detect oil and other minerals underground, the depth, quantity and quality, and will reduce the number of misses or dry holes. Archaeologists, meteorologists, metallurgists, and others will use clairvoyance in their specialties to gather more information that will help them improve the quality of their work.

The astronomer will find he can use his clairvoyant mind to explore the universe much more economically than by launching spacecraft. The same can be said for the human who at some time or other must travel from one inhabited planet to another, and who leaves the body behind and acquires a new body more suited for that environment. The clairvoyant astronomer may also find other civilizations that reside in other dimensions on this and other planets and satellites, civilizations that cannot be detected with our limited objective senses, because these civilizations can exist at other channeled frequencies that require a different set of sensing faculties.

Industrialists will be able to use clairvoyance to better determine what to manufacture for future consumption. Stock-market specialists and investors can use clairvoyance to mentally project into the future and sense the future needs of the population so as to make the correct choice of stocks that will have the greatest demand. Financiers can use clairvoyance to make the best decisions on what projects to invest in. Through their clairvoyance, they can determine which potential projects will provide the greatest service to humanity and thus help make this world a better place to live while earning enough money for their own needs in the process.

Pilots and operators of all types of vehicles will use clairvoyance to free themselves from accidents. When a person functions at his clairvoyant level, not only does he strengthen his immune system, but he also strengthens his intuitive factor, which is a function of the right brain hemisphere. A person with a very strong intuitive factor will subconsciously move, function, or act in a timely way to escape dangers. Consequently, I say people who are not clairvoyant have no business operating vehicles, endangering their own lives and the lives of others.

Ranchers and farmers, who are responsible for providing the food for human survival, will use clairvoyance to select proper breeds and proper seeds to use. In other words, they will be better able to select the best of everything used in the production of food for the human race on this planet.

Parents are the only ones really responsible for the continuation of the existence of the human race on this planet. They serve as doorways through which humans enter this planet. Parents should be the newcomers' fundamental teachers, models, and guides.

We call the newcomers our sons and daughters, but they are not ours; they don't belong to us. They are only placed in our charge. We have been selected to play the role of consultants and guides for them, and to care for them and supply all their needs. It is going to cost us just as much to care for them as it cost our parents to care for us. This is how we pay the system back for what we cost our parents.

All humans arriving on this planet have been sent by the same power for the same purpose by the same means, and regardless of what we have called race, creed, or color, the whole world is their home.

We who have come before them took it upon ourselves to define and establish borders so that newcomers to the planet may or may not cross those borders.

Keep in mind that newcomers to this planet are traveling on their own path in the universe and arrive on this planet individually. After their short stay, they leave this planet individually and again continue traveling on their own path in the universe. Nobody belongs to anybody. We all belong to our Creator, and we are here to help our Creator in the molding of creation.

The titles of fathers and mothers are given to the ones who are to take care of the newcomers to the planet, and to care for them until they are capable of caring for themselves. The fatherly and motherly love that we manifest to the newcomers to this planet is a program established within us by our Creator to abide by our obligation to take care of them.

Why are we to play the roles of teachers, models, and guides? Simply because we got here first and should know our way around and should also know what direction we should guide them in. It is our obligation to guide them correctly in the direction they should take; this is the responsibility we have towards our Creator.

All parents need to be, and should be, clairvoyants. We need to use these intuitive and prophetic abilities to properly guide the newcomers of this planet. It is our obligation towards our Creator, remember? We have a tendency to forget it.

My recommendation for humans who desire to be parents is, first, to be trained in clairvoyance so you will have a better chance to be correct on the selection of the person who is to be your lifetime partner. Nonclairvoyants are only 20 percent accurate when selecting. No wonder there are so many divorces. On the other hand, the clairvoyant who has practiced clairvoyance can be 80 percent accurate or better. Of course, this helps in selecting the correct lifetime partner. People who practice living together before marriage manifest the nonuse of either brain hemisphere; some keep on changing partners until perhaps they find the right one. Some animals have better systems than this.

The child's best teacher and programmer is always the child's mother. The female, by nature, is always more spiritual and more intuitive. Clairvoyant parents can help their clairvoyant sons and daughters, through the use of clairvoyance, to correct bad habits and establish good ones. They also teach them to develop their own control, so that nobody will ever control them and put them to work as slaves selling candy, flowers, and books in airports and on street corners.

A very important message for parents is to remember that whoever gets into your child's brain and mind first is the winner. So, parents, be sure that you, to be the winners, get into the minds and brains of your sons and daughters first through the use of clairvoyance. This will make the child the real winner.

Now we have walked together through my memories of the past, and have stood together and taken a peek at the future from the threshold of the second phase of human evolution on this planet. The next step on this journey belongs to all of us together, the seven billion plus of us on this planet who are developing our clairvoyant abilities so that we can truly make this world a better place to live.

We are the pioneers of this new phase of human evolution, we seven billion plus who are developing the new science of psycho-rientology on this planet, the science of tomorrow—today. Our immediate goal is to bring these research findings to as many people as possible in the shortest possible time.

Now I have shared with you my discoveries. It is time for you to make your own discoveries, as you practice and learn to use your clairvoyant abilities. As we say to people who have never done it, "The greatest discovery you will ever make is the discovery of the potential of your own mind."

Who Are You?

My esteemed colleague and Silva lecturer Harry McKnight has a way of asking his students: "Who are you?" so that the answer is inherent in the question.

The students have already demonstrated their clairvoyant ability by working health cases. He points out what they were able to do.

"When you are able to project your intelligence any distance, that is the quality of being infinite. When you can go forward or backward in time—eternal. When you can know something you have no way of knowing—omniscient. When you are able to correct problems or abnormalities—omnipotent."

Then comes the question. "Infinite, eternal, omniscient, omnipotent: who are you?"

You can hear a pin drop.

Whoever you are, you and higher intelligence are connected. All the great sages proclaimed in their own way that "I and the Father are one."

In Buddhism: "Look within, thou art Buddha."

In Hinduism: "Atman (individual consciousness) and Brahman (universal consciousness) are one."

In Christianity: "The kingdom of God is within you."

In the Upanishads, we read: "By understanding the Self all this universe is known."

Muhammad said: "He who knows himself knows his Lord."

I am honored to know you, clairvoyant businessperson. But more importantly, you should be honored to know yourself. You honor your body, you honor your family, you honor your company and, we hope, your country and your world.

It is my personal wish that you also honor higher intelligence, and that higher intelligence be grateful for your support.

The world is full of unfinished projects. We need to work on protecting the environment, on control of nuclear weapons, on hunger, on preservation of the species.

Excuse me, what did you say? You have a staff meeting in 30 minutes, and you wish to reinforce your programming for a successful outcome? Of course. I'll leave you. You have my warmest wishes.

5 − 4 − 3 − 2 − 1 . . .

Appendix A

The Silva Centering Exercise
BY JOSÉ SILVA

The Silva Centering Exercise helps you discover an inner dimension, a dimension that you can use to become healthier, luckier, and more successful in achieving your goals.

When you learn to function from this inner dimension, you automatically become more spiritual, more human, healthier, safer from accidents, and a more successful problem solver.

In order for you to use this inner dimension, you need to hear the Silva Centering Exercise for a total of 10 hours, and to follow the simple directions in the mind exercise.

How to Read the Silva Centering Exercise
When reading the Silva Centering Exercise, read in a relaxed, natural voice. Be close enough so that the listener can hear you comfortably. Read loud enough to be heard, and read as though

you were reading to a seven-year-old child. Speak each word clearly and distinctly.

Have the listener assume a comfortable position. A sitting position is preferred, but the most important thing is to make sure the listener is comfortable. If uncomfortable, the listener will not relax as much and will not get as much benefit from the exercise.

Avoid distractions, such as loud outside noises. There should be enough light so you can read comfortably, but not extremely bright lights.

If the person shows any signs of nervousness or appears to be uncomfortable, stop reading and tell them to relax and make themselves comfortable. When they are comfortable and ready, then continue.

Take your time when you read; there is no need to rush.

Deepening: Physical Relaxation at Level 3

Find a comfortable position, close your eyes, take a deep breath, and while exhaling, mentally repeat and visualize the number 3 three times. (pause)

To help you learn to relax physically at level 3, I am going to direct your attention to different parts of your body.

Concentrate your sense of awareness on your scalp, the skin that covers your head; you will detect a fine vibration, a tingling sensation, a feeling of warmth caused by circulation. (pause) Now release and completely relax all tensions and ligament pressures from this part of your head, and place it in a deep state of relaxation that will grow deeper as we continue. (pause)

Concentrate your sense of awareness on your forehead, the skin that covers your forehead; you will detect a fine vibration, a tingling sensation, a feeling of warmth caused by circulation. (pause) Now release and completely relax all tensions and ligament pressures from this part of your head, and place it in a deep state of relaxation that will grow deeper as we continue. (pause)

Concentrate your sense of awareness on your eyelids and the tissue surrounding your eyes; you will detect a fine vibration, a tingling sensation, a feeling of warmth caused by circulation. (pause) Now release and completely relax all tensions and ligament pressures from this part of your head, and place it in a deep state of relaxation that will grow deeper as we continue. (pause)

Concentrate your sense of awareness on your face, the skin covering your cheeks; you will detect a fine vibration, a tingling sensation, a feeling of warmth caused by circulation. (pause) Now release and completely relax all tensions and ligament pressures from this part of your head, and place it in a deep state of relaxation that will grow deeper as we continue. (pause)

Concentrate on the outer portion of your throat, the skin covering your throat area; you will detect a fine vibration, a tingling sensation, a feeling of warmth caused by circulation. (pause) Now release and completely relax all tensions and ligament pressures from this part of your body, and place it in a deep state of relaxation that will grow deeper as we continue. (pause)

Concentrate within the throat area, relax all tensions and ligament pressures from this part of your body, and place it in a deep state of relaxation, going deeper and deeper every time. (pause)

Concentrate on your shoulders; feel your clothing in contact with your body. (pause) Feel the skin and the vibration of the skin covering this part of your body. (pause) Relax all tensions and ligament pressures, and place your shoulders in a deep state of relaxation, going deeper and deeper every time. (pause)

Concentrate on your chest; feel your clothing in contact with this part of your body. (pause) Feel the skin and the vibration of your skin covering your chest. (pause) Relax all tensions and ligament pressures, and place your chest in a deep state of relaxation, going deeper and deeper every time. (pause)

Concentrate within the chest area; relax all organs; relax all glands; relax all tissues, including the cells themselves, and cause them to function in a rhythmic, healthy manner. (pause)

Concentrate on your abdomen; feel the clothing in contact with this part of your body. (pause) Feel the skin and the vibration of your skin covering your abdomen. (pause) Relax all tensions and ligament pressures, and place your abdomen in a deep state of relaxation, going deeper and deeper every time. (pause)

Concentrate within the abdominal area; relax all organs; relax all glands; relax all tissues, including the cells themselves, and cause them to function in a rhythmic, healthy manner. (pause)

Concentrate on your thighs; feel your clothing in contact with this part of your body. (pause) Feel the skin and the vibration of your skin covering your thighs. (pause) Relax all tensions and ligament pressures, and place your thighs in a deep state of relaxation, going deeper and deeper every time. (pause)

Sense the vibrations at the bones within the thighs; by now these vibrations should be easily detectable. (pause)

Concentrate on your knees; feel the skin and the vibration of your skin covering the knees. (pause) Relax all tensions and ligament pressures, and place your knees in a deep state of relaxation, going deeper and deeper every time (pause)

Concentrate on your calves; feel the skin and the vibration of the skin covering your calves. (pause) Relax all tensions and ligament pressures, and place these parts of your body in a deep state of relaxation, going deeper and deeper every time. (pause)

To enter a deeper, healthier level of mind, concentrate on your toes. (pause) Enter a deeper, healthier level of mind.

To enter a deeper, healthier level of mind, concentrate on the soles of your feet. (pause) Enter a deeper, healthier level of mind. (pause)

To enter a deeper, healthier level of mind, concentrate on the heels of your feet. (pause) Enter a deeper, healthier level of mind. (pause)

Now cause your feet to feel as though they do not belong to your body. (pause)

Feel your feet as though they do not belong to your body. (pause)

Your feet feel as though they do not belong to your body. (pause)

Your feet, ankles, calves, and knees feel as though they do not belong to your body. (pause)

Your feet, ankles, calves, knees, thighs, waist, shoulders, arms, and hands feel as though they do not belong to your body. (pause)

You are now at a deeper, healthier level of mind, deeper than before.

This is your physical relaxation level 3. Whenever you mentally repeat and visualize the number 3, your body will relax as completely as you are now, and more so every time you practice.

Deepening: Mental Relaxation at Level 2

To enter the mental relaxation level 2, mentally repeat and visualize the number 2 several times, and you are at level 2, a deeper level than 3. (pause) Level 2 is for mental relaxation, where noises will not distract you. Instead, noises will help you to relax mentally more and more.

To help you learn to relax mentally at level 2, I am going to call your attention to different passive scenes. Visualizing any scene that makes you tranquil and passive will help you relax mentally.

Your being at the beach on a nice summer day may be a tranquil and passive scene for you. (pause)

A day out fishing may be a tranquil and passive scene for you. (pause) A tranquil and passive scene for you may be a walk through the woods on a beautiful summer day, when the breeze is just right, where there are tall shade trees, beautiful flowers, a very blue sky, an occasional white cloud, birds singing in the distance, even squirrels playing on the tree limbs. Hear birds singing in the distance. (pause) This is mental relaxation level 2, where noises will not distract you.

To enhance mental relaxation at level 2, practice visualizing tranquil and passive scenes.

To Enter Your Center

To enter level 1, mentally repeat and visualize the number 1 several times. (pause)

You are now at level 1, the basic level where you can function from your center.

Deepening Exercises

To enter deeper, healthier levels of mind, practice with the count-down deepening exercises.

To deepen, count down from 25 to 1, or from 50 to 1, or from 100 to 1. When you reach the count of 1, you will have reached a deeper, healthier level of mind, deeper than before.

You will always have full control and complete dominion over your faculties and senses at all levels of the mind, including the outer conscious level.

When to Practice

The best time to practice the countdown deepening exercises is in the morning, when you wake up. Remain in bed for at least five minutes practicing the countdown deepening exercises.

The second best time to practice is at night, when you are ready to retire.

The third best time to practice is at noon after lunch.

Five minutes of practice is good; 10 minutes is very good; 15 minutes is excellent.

To practice once a day is good; two times a day is very good; and three times a day is excellent.

If you have a health problem, practice for 15 minutes three times a day.

To Come out of Levels

To come out of any level of the mind, count to yourself mentally from 1 to 5 and tell yourself that at the count of 5 you will open your eyes, be wide awake, feeling fine and in perfect health, feeling better than before.

Then proceed to count slowly from 1 to 2, then to 3, and at the count of 3 mentally remind yourself that at the count of 5 you will open your eyes, be wide awake, feeling fine and in perfect health, feeling better than before.

Proceed to count slowly to 4, then to 5. At the count of 5 and with your eyes open, mentally tell yourself, "I am wide awake, feeling fine, and in perfect health, feeling better than before. And this is so."

Deepening: Routine Cycle

To help you enter a deeper, healthier level of mind, I am going to count from 10 to 1. On each descending number, you will feel yourself going deeper, and you will enter a deeper, healthier level of mind.

10 – 9, feel going deeper,

8 – 7 – 6, deeper and deeper,

5 – 4 – 3, deeper and deeper,

2 – 1

You are now at a deeper, healthier level of mind, deeper than before.

You may enter a deeper, healthier level of mind by simply relaxing your eyelids. Relax your eyelids. (pause) Feel how relaxed they are. (pause) Allow this feeling of relaxation to flow slowly downward throughout your body, all the way down to your toes. (pause)

It is a wonderful feeling to be deeply relaxed, a very healthy state of being.

To help you enter a deeper, healthier level of mind, I am going to count from 1 to 3. At that moment, you will project yourself mentally to your ideal place of relaxation. I will then stop talking to you, and when you next hear my voice, one hour of time will have elapsed at this level of mind. My voice will not startle you; you will take a deep breath, relax, and go deeper.

1 – (pause) – 2 – (pause) – 3.

Project yourself mentally to your ideal place of relaxation until you hear my voice again. Relax. (Lecturer: remain silent for about 30 seconds.) Relax. (pause) Take a deep breath, and as you exhale, relax and go deeper. (pause)

Rapport

You will continue to listen to my voice; you will continue to follow the instructions at this level of the mind and any other level, including the outer conscious level. This is for your benefit; you desire it, and it is so.

Whenever you hear me mention the word "Relax," all unnecessary movements and activities of your body, brain, and mind will cease immediately, and you will become completely passive and relaxed physically and mentally.

I may bring you out of this level or a deeper level than this by counting to you from 1 to 5. At the count of 5, your eyes will open; you will be wide awake, feeling fine and in perfect health.

I may bring you out of this level or a deeper level than this by touching your left shoulder three times. When you feel my hand touch your left shoulder for the third time, your eyes will open; you will be wide awake, feeling fine and in perfect health. And this is so.

Genius Statements

The difference between genius mentality and lay mentality is that geniuses use more of their minds and use them in a special manner.

You are now learning to use more of your mind and to use it in a special manner.

Beneficial Statements

The following are beneficial statements that you may occasionally repeat while at these levels of the mind. Repeat mentally after me. (Lecturer: Read slowly.)

My increasing mental faculties are for serving humanity better.

Every day, in every way, I am getting better, better, and better.

Positive thoughts bring me benefits and advantages I desire.

I have full control and complete dominion over my sensing faculties at this level of the mind and at any other level, including the outer conscious level. And this is so.

I will always maintain a perfectly healthy body and mind.

Effective Sensory Projection Statements

I am now learning to attune my intelligence by developing my sensing faculties and to project them to any problem area so as to be aware of any actions taking place, if this is necessary and beneficial for humanity.

I am now learning to correct any problems I detect.

Negative thoughts and negative suggestions have no influence over me at any level of the mind.

Post Effects: Preview of Next Session

You have practiced entering deep, healthy levels of mind. In your next session, you will enter a deeper, healthier level of mind, faster and easier than this time.

Post Effects: Standard

Every time you function at these levels of the mind, you will receive beneficial effects physically and mentally.

You may use these levels of the mind to help yourself physically and mentally.

You may use these levels of the mind to help your loved ones, physically and mentally.

You may use these levels of the mind to help any human being who needs help, physically and mentally.

You will never use these levels of the mind to harm any human being; if this be your intention, you will not be able to function within these levels of the mind.

You will always use these levels of the mind in a constructive, creative manner for all that is good, honest, pure, clean, and positive. And this is so.

You will continue to strive to take part in constructive and creative activities to make this a better world to live in, so that when we move on, we shall have left behind a better world for those who follow. You will consider the whole of humanity, depending on their ages, as fathers or mothers, brothers or sisters, sons or daughters. You are a superior human being; you have greater understanding, compassion, and patience with others.

Bring Out

In a moment, I am going to count from 1 to 5. At that moment, you will open your eyes, be wide awake, feeling fine and in perfect health, feeling better than before. You will have no ill effects whatsoever in your head, no headache; no ill effects whatsoever in your hearing, no buzzing in your ears; no ill effects whatsoever in your vision and eyesight; vision, eyesight, and hearing improve every time you function at these levels of mind.

1 – 2, coming out slowly now.

3, at the count of 5, you will open your eyes, be wide awake, feeling fine and in perfect health, feeling better than before, feeling the way you feel when you have slept the right amount of revitalizing, refreshing, relaxing, healthy sleep.

4 – 5, eyes open, wide awake, feeling fine and in perfect health, feeling better than before.

(Reader: be sure to observe whether or not the person is wide awake. If in doubt, touch the person's left shoulder three times and while doing so, say: "Wide awake, feeling fine and in perfect health. And this is so.")

It is recommended that everyone practice staying at their center for 15 minutes a day to normalize all abnormal conditions of the body and mind.

Appendix B

The Forty-Day Countdown System for
Finding the Alpha Level

I will give you a simple way to relax, and you will do better and better at this as you practice.

I will also give you a beneficial statement to help you.

This is how you train your mind. You relax, lower your brain frequency to the alpha level, and practice using imagination and visualization.

Because you cannot read this book and relax simultaneously, it is necessary that you read the instructions first, so that you can put the book down, close your eyes, and follow them.

Here they are:

1. Sit comfortably in a chair and close your eyes. Any position that is comfortable is a good position.
2. Take a deep breath, and as you exhale, relax your body.

3. Count backward slowly from 50 to 1.

4. Daydream about some peaceful place you know.

5. Say to yourself mentally, "Every day, in every way, I am getting better, better, and better."

6. Remind yourself mentally that when you open your eyes at the count of 5, you will feel wide awake, better than before. When you reach the count of 3, repeat this, and when you open your eyes, repeat it: "I am wide awake, feeling better than before."

You already know steps one and two. You do them daily when you get home in the evening. Add a countdown, a peaceful scene, and a beneficial statement to help you become better and better, and you are ready for a final count-out.

Read the instructions once more. Then put the book down and do it.

Learning to Function Consciously at the Alpha Level

As stated previously, you learn to enter the alpha level and function there with just one day of training when you attend the Silva UltraMind ESP Systems live training programs. You can use the audio recordings to learn to enter the alpha level within a few days with either a Silva home study program or the free lessons at the www.SilvaNow.com website. You can also record the Silva Centering Exercise in appendix A and listen to it, or have someone read it to you.

If you have already learned to enter the alpha level by one of those methods, you can skip the following instructions for practicing countdown-deepening exercises for the next 40 days.

If not, then follow these instructions from José Silva:

When you enter sleep, you enter alpha. But you quickly go right through alpha to the deeper levels of theta and delta.

Throughout the night, your brain moves back and forth through alpha, theta, and delta, like the ebb and flow of the tide. These cycles last about 90 minutes.

In the morning, as you exit sleep, you come out through alpha, back into the faster beta frequencies that are associated with the outer conscious levels.

Some authors advise that as you go to sleep at night, you think about your goals. That way, you get a little bit of alpha time for programming. The only trouble is, you have a tendency to fall asleep.

For now, I just want you to practice a simple exercise that will help you learn to enter and stay at the alpha level. Then, in 40 days, you will be ready to begin your programming.

In the meantime, I will give you some additional tasks that you can perform at the beta level. They will help you prepare yourself so that you will be able to program more effectively at the alpha level when you are ready at the completion of the 40 days.

Your First Assignment

If you are using the Silva Centering Exercise (also known as the Long Relaxation Exercise) on the www.SilvaNow.com website to enter the alpha level, then you can skip the information that follows.

If you do not want to use the recording of the Silva Centering Exercise, and you have not attended a Silva seminar or used one of our home study courses to learn to enter the alpha level, then you will need to follow the instructions here to learn to enter the alpha level on your own.

Here is your alpha exercise:

Practice this exercise in the morning when you first wake up. Since your brain is starting to shift from alpha to beta when you first wake up, you will not have a tendency to fall asleep when you enter alpha.

Here are the steps to take:

1. When you awake tomorrow morning, go to the bathroom if you have to, then go back to bed. Set your alarm clock to ring in 15 minutes, just in case you do fall asleep again.

2. Close your eyes and turn them slightly upward toward your eyebrows (about 20 degrees). Research shows that this produces more alpha brain-wave activity.

3. Count backward slowly from 100 to 1. Do this silently; that is, do it mentally to yourself. Wait about 1 second between numbers.

4. When you reach the count of 1, hold a mental picture of yourself as a success. An easy way to do this is to recall the most recent time when you were 100 percent successful. Recall the setting, where you were, and what the scene looked like; recall what you did; and recall what you felt like.

5. Repeat mentally, "Every day in every way I am getting better, better, and better."

6. Then say to yourself, "I am going to count from 1 to 5; when I reach the count of 5, I will open my eyes, feeling fine and in perfect health, feeling better than before."

7. Begin to count. When you reach 3, repeat, "When I reach the count of 5, I will open my eyes, feeling fine and in perfect health, feeling better than before."

8. Continue your count to 4 and 5. At the count of 5, open your eyes and tell yourself mentally, "I am wide awake, feeling fine and in perfect health, feeling better than before. And this is so."

These Eight Steps Are Really Only Three

Go over each of these eight steps so that you understand the purpose, while at the same time becoming more familiar with the sequence.

1. The mind cannot relax deeply if the body is not relaxed. It is better to go to the bathroom and permit your body to enjoy full comfort. Also, when you first awake, you may not be fully awake. Going to the bathroom ensures that you will be fully awake. But in case you are still not awake enough to stay awake, set your alarm clock to ring in 15 minutes so that you do not risk being late on your daily schedule. Sit in a comfortable position.

2. Research has shown that when a person turns the eyes up about 20 degrees, it triggers more alpha rhythm in the brain and also causes more right-brain activity. Later, when we do our mental picturing, it will be with your eyes turned upward at this angle. Meanwhile, it is a simple way to encourage alpha brain-wave activity. You might want to think of the way you look up at the screen in a movie theater, a comfortable upward angle.

3. Counting backward is relaxing. Counting forward is activating: 1–2–3 is like "get ready, get set, go!" while 3–2–1 is pacifying. You are going nowhere except deeper within yourself.

4. While you are relaxed, imagining yourself the way you want to be creates the picture. Failures who relax and imagine themselves making mistakes and losing frequently create a mental picture that brings about failure. You will do the opposite. Your mental picture is one of success, and it will create what you desire: success.

5. Words repeated mentally—while you are relaxed—create the concepts they stand for. Pictures and words program the mind to make it so.

6–8. These last three steps are simply counting to 5 to end your session. Counting upward activates you, but it's still good to give yourself "orders" to become activated at the count of 5. Do this before you begin to count; do it again along the way; and again as you open your eyes.

Once you wake up tomorrow morning and prepare yourself for this exercise, it all works down to three steps:

1. Count backward from 100 to 1.
2. Imagine yourself successful.
3. Count yourself out 1 to 5, reminding yourself that you are wide awake, feeling fine, and in perfect health.

Forty Days That Can Change Your Life for the Better

You know what to do tomorrow morning, but what about after that? Here is your training program:

Count backward from 100 to 1 for 10 mornings.

Count backward from 50 to 1 for 10 mornings.

Count backward from 25 to 1 for 10 mornings.

Count backward from 10 to 1 for 10 mornings.

After these 40 mornings of countdown relaxation practice, count backward only from 5 to 1 and begin to use your alpha level.

People have a tendency to be impatient, to want to move faster. Please resist this temptation and follow the instructions as written.

You must develop and acquire the ability to function consciously at alpha before the mental techniques will work properly for you. You must master the fundamentals first. We've been researching this field since 1944, longer than anyone else, and the techniques we have developed have helped millions of people worldwide to enjoy greater success and happiness, so please follow these simple instructions.

Appendix C

ESP for Executives

BY JOHN MIHALASKY, ED.D.

In the last few years it has become increasingly difficult for business and industry to stay competitive. Critics charge that there is too much reliance on short-term thinking and on the fear of taking risks.

With more data being generated by more and more computers, there has been a tendency to slip into a posture of "managing by the numbers." The emphasis has been on the use of rationality and logic in problem solving and decision making—operations research, management science, modeling, and the development of computers that "think."

Unfortunately, all this has given us more and more incorrect, invalid, and/or unreliable data faster, leading us to make decisions whose outcomes have been correct about as many times as those made by holding a wet finger up to the wind.

It is my contention that this state of affairs is due to the fact that not enough has been done to investigate the application of illogical, nonrational, unconscious thinking. We have spent most of our time on rational, logical, conscious thinking. It is (and has been for a long time) necessary to delve into the use of the unconscious.

The purpose of the material in this chapter is to explore the basis for the use of the unconscious—ESP, if you will—in the problem-solving and decision-making processes.

The Precognitive Decision Maker

The PSI Communications Project at the Newark College of Engineering (now the New Jersey Institute of Technology) researched the phenomenon of precognition and the nature of the precognitive decision maker in the 1960s and 1970s.

There is now evidence to suggest that the successful "hunch player"—a person who makes decisions based on hunches rather than fact or evidence—may have something more solid going for him or her than the odds of chance.

Experiments indicate that what the texts call illogical (and what managers privately call "lucky") decisions have some scientific—that is, observable, dependable, and explainable—support.

The research project strongly supports the idea that some executives have more precognitive ability than others—that is, they are better able to anticipate the future intuitively rather than logically, and thus, when put in positions where strong data support may not always exist, will make better decisions.

Moreover, a valid test has been developed for determining which people do, and which do not, have this ability.

The test consists of asking the participants to guess at a 100-digit number not currently in existence. (The numbers would later be computer-generated using random-number techniques.) Each of the 100 digits can take on any value from zero to nine. A computer generates a specific target for each participant.

As expected, some people guess above the chance level of 10 correct guesses out of the 100 digits, while others guess at, or below, the chance level.

That some people score above chance on this test would not, by itself, prove they have precognitive ability. But the research has revealed some interesting and significant relationships between high scores on this simple guessing game and other kinds of data.

For example, participants are asked to rank their preferences among five metaphors (such as "a motionless ocean," "a dashing horseman," and so forth) that have been adapted from a psychological test.

Based on their choices, the subjects are divided into *dynamic* and *nondynamic* types. Admittedly, this is not a very sophisticated classification. But invariably, those classified as dynamic by this relatively simple means also tend to score above chance in predicting the computer's random numbers.

In tests on 27 different groups, ranging from four members to 100, dynamic people outscored nondynamic people in 22 of the groups. Statistically, the chances of this happening by accident are fewer than 5 in 1000. Many other groups were tested after this initial 27.

But what does a dynamic executive mean? Whatever it connotes, it must also be measured somehow by performance.

Four groups of chief operating officers of corporations, all of them in their present jobs for at least five years, were asked to take the tests. These men had held office long enough to assume responsibility for the reliability of their decisions and the recent performance of their companies.

The first two groups of chief executives were divided into two classes: those who had at least doubled profits in the past five years, and those who had not. The second group included some who had lost money.

Of the 12 men whose companies doubled their profits, 11 scored above the chance level on the computer guessing game. One scored at the chance level, and not a single one fell below chance.

Of the 13 who had *not* doubled profits, seven scored below chance, one scored at chance, and five scored above chance. This last five had improved profits by 50 to 100 percent. Of the seven who scored below chance, five had improved profits less than 50 percent. Only two of those who scored below chance had improved profits more substantially than that.

The chief executives who had more than doubled their companies' profits in five years had an average score of 12.8 correct guesses out of 100. Those who had not met this criteria scored an average of 8.3, well below what they should have achieved even on a random basis.

To give one striking example of the difference between the two groups: Over a five-year period, one president had increased his company's annual profit from $1.3 million to $19.4 million. His test score was 16. Another had been able to increase his profit by only $374,000. His score was 8.

The third group of participants consisted of 41 members of the Association of Steel Distributors. Of the 41, 11 had been company presidents for at least five years. Of those 11, 9 had at least doubled their companies' profits over the last five years. Eight of these 9 scored above chance. Their average was 11.44 percent. The remaining 2, who had not at least doubled their company profits, averaged 9.5 percent, with both scoring at chance or less.

The fourth group was composed of 20 Canadian businesspeople. Of them, 6 had been company presidents in their current jobs for at least five years. Five of the 6 at least doubled the profits, while one fell into the 50 to 95 percent improvement class. Of the five profit-doublers, 3 scored above chance; the other 2 were below chance. The sixth person scored at chance level.

This finding has interesting implications for selection of executives for the top spot. Given a group of people who have the usual traits needed for such a position, which one should be selected?

I feel that it should be the person with the something extra—in this case, the ability to make good decisions under conditions of uncertainty.

In the groups of company presidents tested, had the selection been made on the basis of their scores, there would have been an 81.5 percent chance of choosing a person who at least doubled the company's profits, while if someone who scored below chance had been chosen, there would have been only a 27.3 percent chance of choosing a person who would have doubled the company's profits.

Development of Precognitive Abilities

Precognition is not of mystical origin, but rather is an energy or information transfer using senses currently not recognizable or known. I believe that everyone has this ability. It is thus not a question of having precognitive ability, but rather of developing the use of the precognitive ability we all possess.

Precognitive information comes in many forms—dreams at night, daydreams, flashes, hunches, and gut feelings. The user has to first be aware of these various forms and then look for their appearance.

With precognition abilities, usage sharpens the talent.

With executives, it has been found that they believe in precognition, use it, and then build a rationale to justify the idea they used, or the decision they made, so as not to look foolish.

Precognitive information is usually obtained concerning a matter in which the problem solver has been deeply and emotionally involved. It also tends to arrive at times when the mind is supposedly resting and not thinking specifically about the problem.

Problem solvers accept and use such information to make decisions, find solutions, and form ideas. There are many engineers and scientists, but the number of those who can come up with good ideas is very small.

These superior idea generators review the same hard data that others have, but they must contribute something extra to come up with their ideas. Part of this something extra may be their ability to gather information through what is loosely called ESP.

The Utilization of Precognitive Ability

Research on precognition ability does not support the idea that this ability is a unique trait. However, it does support the idea that some people have more of this ability—and make better use of it—than others.

The executive who wishes to avail himself of the ability to use precognition must first understand the nature and form of this phenomenon.

Precognition is a part of the unconscious process. As such, it is not bound by the usual limitations of space and time.

The ideal condition for the utilization of precognition information is when it does not require decoding or interpretation. The interpretation process, which tends to be logical and rational, can rework the illogical, but incorrect, information.

An example of getting precognition information would be the sudden thought that comes to an automobile driver to take a side road rather than the usual straight and shorter highway. The thought is not heeded, and later on down the highway, the motorist runs into a traffic jam.

Sir Winston Churchill is reported to have had a "feeling" that caused him to sit on the side of the car that he never used. Later on, as the auto was speeding down the road, a bomb exploded, causing the auto to rise up on two side wheels. Because of Churchill's weight, the auto did not turn over but righted itself. Had Churchill not heeded the information that came to him, he would probably have been killed.

The executives studied not only had to be able to recognize the format of precognition information, but they also had to be prepared to get it any time. For them, this was not an ability that could be turned on and off at will.

Next, the user of precognitive information has to have the faith and guts to use it. It is necessary to accept the existence of the phenomenon, whether or not the user knows how or why it happens.

Finally, the "practice makes perfect" rule should be followed. The intuitive decision maker has to make using precognition information a habit.

Each decision maker has to test the existence of precognition for himself with an open and positive mental attitude.

If you deny its existence, you are, in effect, repressing it, and it will go away. We tend, out of fear, to resist anything we do not understand. Our research indicates that the best results were achieved when resistance was at a minimum. For ESP abilities to function, we have to overcome any resistance we may have.

Several individuals I know had precognitive abilities, were frightened of them, and ultimately managed to suppress them. When they realized that the ability could be very useful, a more relaxed attitude resulted, and the ability began to return.

Common sense dictates that in any situation where knowledge is incomplete, the approach should be gentle. This is probably the best advice one can offer concerning precognition.

Be willing to believe that it exists. Have the courage to use it.

What Inhibits Precognition

Do not expect to get good intuitive action under stressful conditions. When test subjects are under stress, the results follow the inverse hypothesis—that is, the dynamic managers who should have scored above chance did not do so. In fact, they scored below chance.

Similarly, you should not expect good results when you are tired or physically under par. Precognition tests consistently indicate that better results are achieved when tests are held early in the day.

Alcohol may also impair precognitive ability. After a three-martini lunch, dynamics from a group of production engineers scored 9.9 on average, and nondynamics scored 9.3 on average. The entire group, in other words, scored below chance. While we cannot with certainty blame the martinis, much evidence already exists concerning alcohol's effect on mental processes. I would suspect that ESP is no exception.

Lastly, you should probably try not to make intuitive decisions in any environment where you feel dominated. If you do, it is possible you may "intentionally" predict the future incorrectly.

It appears that if you are assured of a dominant role in the environment, and have precognitive ability, you will probably score high, almost as if validating the status quo. We call this the *dominance effect*.

But if your role is a dominated one, you may reinforce the existing hierarchical structure by "deliberately" scoring low.

During tests with mixed-sex groups, the dominating sex validated the hypothesis: dynamics scored higher than nondynamics. But the dominated sex produced a mirror image—that is, dynamics scored lower.

In another case, executives or owners who were fathers or fathers-in-law dominated their sons and sons-in-law. (By dominance we do not mean numerical superiority. It might better be termed *environmental*.)

In tests in groups where the environment was discernibly dominated by one sex, the dominance effect was noted. In groups where the sexes met on an equal footing, there was no mirror imaging or following of the inverse hypothesis.

Professor Emeritus John Mihalasky, Ed.D., taught industrial engineering at The New Jersey Institute of Technology (formerly Newark College of Engineering) for 31 years. He was the director of the PSI Communications Project. After he retired in 1987, he continued to teach part-time. He is one of the authors of Executive ESP *(Prentice Hall, 1974), the book about the landmark research project on precognition. He died in 2006 after a long and distinguished career.*

Appendix D

Resources and Contact Information

FREE INTRODUCTORY LESSONS
www.SilvaNow.com

INFORMATION ABOUT SILVA BOOKS, RECORDINGS, COURSES, AND OTHER PRODUCTS
www.SilvaCourses.com

To contact the authors of this book or any Silva UltraMind ESP Systems instructor, or for a schedule of seminars, please visit the Silva Instructors Website: www.SilvaInstructors.com.

SILVA INTERNATIONAL GRADUATE ASSOCIATION
www.SIGA.org

ECUMENICAL SOCIETY HOLISTIC FAITH HEALING WEBSITE

www.ESPsy.org

If you have a health problem and want Silva graduates to pro-gram for you, or if you are a Silva graduate and want health cases to work, please visit this website:

www.HealthCases.com

JOSÉ SILVA JR.'S WEBSITE

www.SilvaJoseJr.com

KATHERINE SANDUSKY'S WEBSITE

www.SilvaSeminars.com

ED BERND JR. (AVLIS PUBLISHING AND AVLIS PRODUCTIONS INC.)

www.SilvaCourses.com

RAYMON GRACE'S WEBSITE

www.raymongrace.us

Index

Printed in the USA
CPSIA information can be obtained
at www.ICGtesting.com
JSHW012019140824
68134JS00033B/2773